Berlin: Success of a Mission?

BERLIN:
Success of a Mission?

Geoffrey McDermott

HARPER & ROW, PUBLISHERS

New York and Evanston

CONTENTS

The passages from 'Pendennis', April 30, 1961, and September 23, 1962, are quoted by kind permission of *The Observer*.

FOREWORD

by ANTHONY GREENWOOD MP

This is an important book because it is written by a professional diplomat who was actively involved in the German problem at the highest level as British Minister in Berlin—and who, in the summer of 1962, was abruptly and mysteriously recalled by the Foreign Office.

The reasons for his 'retirement' as the Foreign Office call it, seemed unconvincing and inconsistent. I became interested and raised the case in the House. I questioned Mr McDermott searchingly and he answered with the utmost candour.

I also extracted as much information as the Foreign Office saw fit to give. Their spokesmen's candour impressed me less favourably than that of Mr McDermott; I still find the official excuses equivocal and unsubstantiated. And the more the Foreign Office has wriggled the more likely it has' seemed that the real reason for the dismissal lies in the ideas Mr McDermott had evolved about the future of Germany.

During his time as British Minister and Deputy Commandant in Berlin, when Mr McDermott scrupulously carried out Western policy and co-operated loyally with his colleagues at a most critical period, he became aware that the military position of the Americans, the French and ourselves in Berlin is, to use his own word, nonsense; the Red Army could take over Berlin within an hour. This, coupled with the fact that he suspected Dr Adenauer of using Berlin to blackmail his allies, convinced him that a rapid solution must be found. That is how the McDermott plan began.

He proposes an agreement between Russia and the Western powers, renewable after twenty years, that German reunification is their long-term aim. The present frontiers of Germany would be agreed to be definitive, and the German Democratic Republic would be recognised as a separate state. So would Berlin, which could then make agreements with any countries she wished (except West Germany and the GDR) to station their troops in reasonable numbers in the city.

The representatives of the Four Powers would have guaranteed access to Berlin and some important United Nations agencies would be moved there. The *three* German states would then join the United Nations and be signatories to the agreements outlined above. All of this he sees as preparing the way for the application of the Rapacki Plan, and the signing of a non-aggression treaty between NATO and the Warsaw Pact countries.

It is, in fact, a moderate scheme worked out by a practical administrator remarkably free from Cold War prejudices. But how embarrassing it must have been to his more conservative colleagues in Berlin, Bonn and Whitehall. And Mr McDermott paid the price. With scant ceremony he was recalled to London, faced with odd bits of tittle-tattle from men he had thought to be his friends, and told (while being reminded that he could, of course, appeal) of the Foreign Office's proposals about his pension *when*, not *if*, he retired.

How much better it would have been if Government spokesmen, instead of involving themselves in personal recriminations against Mr McDermott, had examined his thesis with the objectivity he himself has brought to bear, and had told us clearly why it was found to be unacceptable.

I do not agree with all of his conclusions. Nor do I accept all his judgments. But I am glad that in this constructive, good-humoured and far-sighted book Mr McDermott has decided to make available to the public at large the views which so clearly embarrassed his superiors and which could provide a useful basis for discussion between East and West.

ANTHONY GREENWOOD

Chapter 1

PRELUDE

When I was told by the Foreign Office in March 1961 that I was to go to Berlin as Minister and Deputy Commandant, I realised that the job would probably be intensely interesting, as a crisis was expected before long. I also knew that I should have to work in a complicated paramilitary framework.

So it turned out; though neither I nor anyone else could then have foreseen the gravity of future events. The crisis provoked by the Communists' Wall was such that nuclear war over Berlin became a threatening possibility. The allied effort to cope with these developments included not only constant, daily collaboration in Berlin with our American and French allies and the Berliners, but similar consultations in Washington, London, Paris, Bonn and Moscow. In such conditions personalities played a large part; especially, in Berlin, those of the Governing Mayor, Willy Brandt, and the personal representative of the United States President, General Lucius D. Clay.

We managed to surmount the crisis, to avoid war and to keep the Western position in Berlin and the morale of the Berliners steady. But in making my contribution to these

9

achievements I unwittingly fell foul of the British Ambassador in Bonn, Sir Christopher Steel, whose deputy I was in my role as Minister; and of Major-General Delacombe, the British Commandant in Berlin, whose deputy I was under my other hat. I do not wish this personal aspect of my time in Berlin to obtrude. It was none of my seeking. But it is part of the story, and I intend to set out the truth.

I took up my post on July 2, 1961. Eleven months later Sir Francis Rundall, the head of administration in the Foreign Office, told me in a letter that complaints had been made against me by Sir Christopher Steel and by Major-General Delacombe, and as a result I was to leave Berlin and be retired from the Foreign Service. It was the first I had heard of any complaints. I was forty-nine years of age at the time and rather high on the Foreign Service seniority list.

This drastic action led, as I shall describe, to publicity both for 'the McDermott plan for Berlin' and for 'the McDermott case'. I aim in this book to set down without malice the story of these developments. I want to help to find a solution for the intolerably dangerous Berlin problem, for I feel it can be solved if only the West will adopt more sensible negotiating methods; and, by relating the circumstances of my dismissal quite objectively I want to throw some light into the darker corners of the Foreign Service so that the Service as a whole may benefit.

My first job in Berlin was to get to know my British colleagues, not only in the office but socially as well. With perhaps a couple of exceptions they were very nice and friendly, and efficient too. Even before my arrival I had had to get to know British policy on Berlin. I had a fortnight's briefing in London in June 1961, when I saw the Foreign Secretary, Lord Home, the Lord Privy Seal, Mr Edward Heath, and the Permanent Under-Secretary at the Foreign Office, as well as those senior officials who were specially concerned with Berlin. We discussed matters at length; but in spite of all their words and the many papers I read on the subject I never really discovered whether or not we had a policy for the future of Berlin. This at least gave us who were on the spot a chance of developing our own policy in response to changing events. We were always careful to keep in step with the other occupying powers, the Americans and the French. I also thought it desirable to keep some lines of communication open with the Russians, though they could seldom be used to much effect. I made a point of calling on the Soviet Commandant and the Soviet Ambassador. These contacts were thought a little unorthodox by some of my colleagues, both British and American, but I am sure they were worth while.

As for the Berliners, there were many most charming people amongst them and a great deal was done through good personal relations with their leading citizens. But we officials were not allowed by our governments to have any contacts with the authorities of the East German Democratic Republic.

Meanwhile, all the time I was brooding on longer-term policy, trying to see whether a solution of the Berlin problem could not be evolved which would improve the position of the West while at the same time making an appeal to the Russians. My ideas were just beginning to take shape when suddenly, without any warning, I was retired from the Service. The Foreign Office view of the 'success' of my mission was clear. I hope in the pages that follow to enable my readers to reach their own conclusion.

Chapter 2

FROM CYPRUS TO BERLIN

I have no regrets at having chosen the Diplomatic Service as my career in life. When, coming down from Cambridge, I took and passed the examinations for both the Diplomatic and the Home Civil Services in 1935, I toyed with the idea of joining the Home Civil (though I had two Firsts in Modern Languages), simply because I thought I would find it easier to enjoy a more normal private life in it. But in fact many civil servants, tied to their desks and committees, look to me as if they never enjoy themselves at all. I have done my stint of office work, both at home and abroad. But I have never thought that diplomacy begins and ends in the office. It is concerned more with people than with pieces of paper, necessary and important though these may sometimes be. I have always liked doing things; I enjoy original and provocative thinking. But, though the general standard of the Foreign Service is as high as ever, I have come to feel the dead hand of Whitehall a great discouragement to those who aspire to originality in thought and action. I have often found the directness and energy of the best type of Service officers, particularly in the Royal Air Force, more congenial than the methods of some of my more conventional colleagues.

I have always been told that I made my name in the succession of posts which I held in the Foreign Office itself during the mid-fifties. In each of them I was concerned with questions of strategy and liaison with the fighting and intelligence services. Most of the work was highly secret, and I got on excellently with the military men and found this collaboration most interesting and enjoyable. It included the detailed planning of the Suez campaign, in which I represented the Foreign Office. In 1956 I was promoted to be the youngest Minister in the Foreign Service. Then, in the summer of 1958, I was appointed Political Representative with the Middle East Forces in Cyprus. At that time the situation on the island was tense and between then and the end of the year, when I was required to arrive, the terrorism increased. But my wife, Elizabeth, never hesitated for a moment about going out with me, and we decided to set up a home as quickly as we could, taking with us our youngest son and his nanny, and two of our other children just for the Christmas holidays.

We arrived on the island, thanks to the courtesy of the Royal Navy, in one of H.M. destroyers, and found ourselves in army quarters looking rather like council houses set down in identical rows with imaginative names like Dorset Drive and Gloucester Hill. As usual in service life these quarters had been allocated strictly by rank and, as my post ranked senior to all major-generals and equivalents, we lived among the top brass. We grew to be very fond of these neighbours of ours, the generals, air marshals and commodores and their families; and there were, of course, many occasions, social and sporting, when we enjoyed the company of servicemen of every rank. Our surroundings could not have been bettered. Climate and landscape alike were attractive. Bathing and tennis were near at hand. Only man was occasionally vile.

By then the worst of the violence was over but the situation was still tense. On the very day of our arrival the Governor, Sir Hugh Foot, had to make the agonising decision whether to reprieve two convicted EOKA murderers in order to encourage a détente or whether to let the death sentence stand and face a probable wave of violence throughout the island. He chose the path of mercy, and there was no widespread violence afterwards, though the situation remained tense. Our life was still shadowed by the fear of terrorism. Whenever Elizabeth drove outside the cantonment to do some shopping she had to be accompanied by an armed soldier, dressed in mufti so as not to attract attention. I myself had to be armed on the longer of my journeys into the interior, and since no one seemed to have much faith in my marksmanship I carried my revolver loaded but in a cardboard box. I remember one of our first diversions after our arrival was a picnic given by the Commander-in-Chief of the Army. It was nicely called an 'armed ramble' because all the service officers taking part had to carry weapons.

At first I was kept pretty busy. In the course of my duties I had to travel all over the area of the Middle East Command and I visited every country on the Mediterranean from Tunis round to Greece, as well as Jordan, Iran and the Persian Gulf. In return we invited our Ambassadors from each of these countries to visit our headquarters, and I helped with the entertaining. I was fully involved in the negotiations with Archbishop Makarios over the independence of Cyprus and the arrangements for the British Sovereign Base Areas. Mr Julian Amery, who handled these negotiations in a masterly manner, was good enough to express to Lord Home his appreciation of my work on this problem.

After more than two years we began to feel that a change of scene would be welcome. For one thing, since Cyprus had become independent in August 1960 our problems in the Base Areas were few, and I had to tell the Foreign Office that I really had not enough work to do. We had also come to feel that we would like a suitable embassy of our own. I was even though nominally a Minister, senior to many ambassadors in the Service. So I entered into correspondence with Sir Francis Rundall and we discussed the possibilities of Venezuela, Hungary and Morocco. All this in a conspicuously friendly way. For one reason or another none of these posts came my way, and in March 1961 they offered me Berlin, as Minister and Deputy Commandant. At first I have to admit that I was not too enthusiastic and I told them so. I would prefer, I said, a straightforward diplomatic post. At this point the pressure was applied. In the jargon of the Service I was told that Berlin would be 'stimulating', 'a challenge'. I was even told that the Ambassador in Bonn and Lord Home himself wanted me there. So I accepted.

The next month Elizabeth and I visited Berlin to make a recce. We began to realise the special nature of the post. Unlike the American and French Governments, the British had never before sent a fully fledged Minister to Berlin, and in a largely military set-up this lack of rank had been a definite handicap. As a result of our visit we were a little more reconciled to making the move by the time we returned to Cyprus. On our way back we stopped off in London and dined with our old friends the Von Herwarths. He was then the German Ambassador: I put him, along with the very different Willy Brandt, among the best Germans I know. He told me how glad he was that I was going to Berlin and very shrewdly advised me to get there by the end of June.

To complete the send-off, the very day we left London *The Observer* printed a short piece under the heading 'Promotion in Berlin', which I quote as it plays quite a part in this story.

'The Foreign Office is upgrading its diplomatic post in Berlin. Unlike his predecessor, GEOFFREY MCDERMOTT, who's to be our New Man there, has the status of Minister.

'He will continue to be known to the public as British Deputy Commandant, but the Commandants, who are military men, are becoming less important than their Deputies, the diplomats—and the number of diplomats in the city is increasing. So McDermott will be pretty well independent; as far as seniority goes he'll come next after SIR CHRISTOPHER STEEL, our Ambassador in Bonn.

'Though the F.O. naturally won't admit it, this looks very much like a sign of the times. After reading WALTER LIPPMANN'S interview with MR KRUSCHEV last week no one can feel confident that the situation in Berlin will stay calm. Either way, however, this appointment looks just the job for McDermott, who's a hot-spot man, who specialised in liaison with the Services for many years. Although he speaks fluent German, no one could say that McDermott was an admirer of the Prussian character. But he has the reputation of getting on well with fighting men; is said to know almost every general in the business.

For the last couple of years he's been political representative with the Middle East Forces based at their H.Q. in Cyprus. There he made a point of living among the troops in their encampment. When SIR HUGH FOOT was negotiating with MAKARIOS he would go down to the camp for advice about bases, and the servicemen liked McDermott to do their talking for them.

'He is forty-nine, a friendly, engaging man and, for an F.O. man, frank to the point of outspokenness. Now that he's been given another tour abroad he and his wife—who is one of the marmalade ROBERTSONS—are selling their large London house. And last week they rushed over to Berlin to find a lakeside house which will hold their five children.

'McDermott plays a good game of tennis, likes swimming and cars. In Cyprus he ordered a white Jaguar for official use, had a red and white Ford convertible of his own. He was rather shocked to find his official car in Berlin was to be a Mercedes, and promptly bought a very pale blue Alvis for the family's use.'

This well-intentioned piece of publicity caused some annoyance in Foreign Office circles, and Sir Christopher Steel, whom I stayed with on my way to Berlin in June, had some harsh things to say of *The Observer*. It is really quite extraordinary how diplomats of the old school still shrink from any reference to the Service even in the most respectable independent journals. I even heard it said by another top official that 'the Foreign Service do not advertise'—as if I had bought the space myself.

Packing up in Cyprus after more than two years there showed us how many friends we had made, and we left for Berlin in June with many tokens of kindness, most notably from the Commander-in-Chief, General Sir Dudley Ward. It was to be a long time before I looked upon his like again. On our arrival we spent a few days with the Delacombes in their very agreeable house on the banks of the Havel. Jumbo, to do him credit, showed no sign of having been put out by *The Observer's* piece, which he might well have interpreted to mean that the Foreign Office was about to take over from

the military. It would, in my view, have been an excellent
thing if they had : but unfortunately the Office are usually
more concerned to preserve the *status quo* and to spare the
feelings of other Services than to stick up for their own.

On our first visit we had been very lucky to hit on a charming house belonging to the Dutch Ambassador, a sort of small
palazzo with a garden reaching down to a little lake on the
edge of the Grunewald. In the past the head British civilian
had always been more modestly housed than his opposite
numbers; and while I personally care not a fig about keeping
up with the Joneses there is no doubt that when it comes to
an official residence these considerations play a part. So I
gladly took the house, where we would be able to entertain in
a suitable manner as well as put up visiting VIPs and personal
friends and family from England. We lived in this house all
our time in Berlin and came to like it very much. Some of my
colleagues were a little dismayed at the amount of marble, but
I did not at all share their view. Indeed, at the risk of sound-
ing sybaritic, I will confess to a special affection for a splendid
sunken marble bath big enough for three. I do not know what
the builder of the house—a Roumanian oil millionaire, we
were led to believe—got up to in that bath; but as good
Government servants we used it strictly for bathing, one person
at a time. (We were rather chagrined to find that one of our
first visitors, James Ramsden, a young Conservative Junior
Minister, had had one in his Yorkshire house for years.)
Another agreeable feature was one of those wooden Turkish
baths out of the top of which only the head appears, very
red, like Colonel Blimp's; but the inside of this contained such
a formidable array of electrical devices that we thought it
safer not to use it. I am happy to add that the British tax-
payer did not have to foot the bill for any of these amiable
fixtures, as all the costs, including the rent, were paid by the

Berlin Administration out of what are still called 'Occupation Costs'.

I can vividly remember the day, July 2, scorchingly hot, when Elizabeth and I, after a brief visit to London, flew into Berlin in a fairly exhausted condition. There had been a technical hitch. Our two Sudanese manservants, who had gone ahead of us from Cyprus, were out for the evening. But a little quick work with the jemmy, and we were able to sleep in our new home. It was the beginning of an eventful year.

Chapter 3

THE BERLIN SET-UP

The Berlin which we now began to get to know was very different from the city we had seen on a visit some seven years before. Owing to the fortitude and industry of the two and a quarter million West Berliners the western part of the city had flourished exceedingly. Rebuilding in the most exciting and impressive modern style had gone ahead fast. What we now saw was a prosperous city, or part-city, with lots of space, excellent roads and buildings, resolute and cheerful people. There was a feeling everywhere of buoyancy and optimism, and trade and employment were booming. How different it had been at the end of the war, when the combined efforts of the allied bombers and the Red Army had reduced the whole place to rubble and Berliners were scraping around for food and survival! One of the gravest blunders made by the Western allies at that time was the decision, basically an American one, to halt the advance on the Elbe instead of marching on Berlin. We had delayed there for weeks while the ponderous Red Army slogged its way into the city. We did this out of a desire to please our Russian ally, but we got little thanks for it. When Germany and Berlin were each divided into four parts the Russians showed no modesty in seizing their share; and from that moment the Soviet zone of Germany, later to be called the German Democratic Republic (GDR), was a communist captive. Under various agreements four-power control was then set up both for Germany as a whole and for Berlin, as well as for the access routes to it across the Soviet zone. These hostages to fortune consist of three air corridors, one road, one railway and one waterway (apart from certain routes not available to the allies). Obviously if all these were closed to allied use West Berlin would sooner or later collapse. Indeed. the Soviet blockade of all surface access routes in 1948–9 seemed almost certain to strangle the city, and it was only the firm stand of the people and the British and American airlift which averted this threatened fate.

The instrument of administration in Berlin was the Allied Kommandatura—a hideous bastard German-Russian term—consisting of the four Commandants and their deputies, plus various sub-committees. In its quadripartite form this had a short and unhappy life, as no Soviet representatives attended its deliberations after 1948. Just as the Western allies then gave Federal Germany her independence step by step and brought her into various alliances culminating in NATO, so the Soviet Government riposted, recognising the independence of the GDR while taking the precaution of bringing her into the Warsaw Pact and thus maintaining the right to station large numbers of Soviet forces on her territory. But whereas the GDR has so far been recognised as an independent state only by members of the communist world, the independence of Federal Germany, first recognised by the Western powers, was soon accepted by many of the communist states as well, the USSR included.

Inside Berlin the three Western allies have preserved the legal fiction of the Kommandatura; and the photograph of the Soviet general who walked out in 1948 is still exhibited in their meeting room, though the photographs and names of the Western commandants change every so often. Until August 1962 the Russians even kept a Soviet commandant in East Berlin to exchange occasional visits with his allied opposite numbers. But almost the only purpose of these visits was to swap protests, of which about ninety-five per cent were rejected out of hand by the recipient, on whichever side. All this time Soviet forces in great strength—reckoned in my time at about twenty-two divisions—and with the most modern armament were stationed within easy reach of Berlin; and at times of crisis, as when General Lucius D. Clay was sent to Berlin by President Kennedy in September 1961 after the building of the Wall, a great Soviet warrior like Marshal Koniev was produced to add weight to their side. For a long time, therefore, the Soviet commandant had been a person of little consequence, and in August last year the post was abolished and the Commander-in-Chief of the Soviet Forces in Germany, General Jakubovsky (who had taken over from Marshal Koniev), officially assumed his functions.

To this day the Western allies, and their forces, remain in Berlin on the basis of the Occupation Statute. The West Berliners are happy to have them there on that basis, since it gives them infinitely better protection than the only alternative—full integration in the Federal Republic. German voices are raised from time to time, both in Berlin and the Federal Republic, in favour of integration, but such a policy, in my view, would be very dangerous. If Berlin were to become an integral part of Federal Germany, the occupation troops would have to go. The city would then either fall a prey to communist subversion and eventual take-over, or Federal German troops would attempt to come to Berlin, a move which the Russians, with good reason, simply would not

allow. The present relationship between Berlin and the Federal
Republic is close and satisfactory, and the 'economic miracle'
has led to Berlin being subsidised in a big way by West Germany. But any move in the direction of integration would be
considered intolerably provocative by the communists. It is
significant that while the allies encourage visits to Berlin by
leading Federal Germans from the President and Chancellor
downwards, despite the complaints of 'provocation' which they
arouse on the other side, we have always refused to allow a
singe Reichswehr officer, even though he is integrated into
NATO, to come to Berlin for any purpose whatever. I am
sure that this is right.

The Berliners call the allies the 'Protecting Powers', and
are on the whole most friendly; while on the allied side the
view is widespread that we are sitting pretty. We have, it is
true, held on to our position successfully under considerable
stress. Kruschev's six-months' ultimatum in 1958, threatening
to hand over to the German Democratic Republic the control
of the access routes which are essential to Berlin's viability,
was weathered without too much difficulty. So was his
attempt to turn the heat on again at his Vienna meeting with
President Kennedy in June 1961.

But are we not in fact sitting on a volcano? In military
terms our position is nonsense. The Americans have some
6,000 troops in Berlin, the British about 3,000, the French
about 2,000; while the Russians, as I have said, have some
twenty-two divisions in East Germany and plenty more
within easy reach. The access routes between the West and
Berlin, which are vital not only to the allies but to the very
life of Berlin itself, could all be severed at a moment's notice,
with the possible exception of the air routes. At one time or
another all the surface routes have been severed; and even
more frequently all routes, including the air routes, have been

Roads ═══ Railways ⫫⫫⫫⫫⫫

Canals ⌒⌒⌒⌒ Airports ◉

Air Corridor ━ ━ ━

P O L A N D

Miles

0   5   10

FRENCH

TEGEL ◉

Wedding ●

Lichtenberg ●

BRITISH

Spandau ●

Brandenburg Gate

RUSSIAN

◉ GATOW

◉ TEMPELHOF

AMERICAN

Lichterfelde ●

Köpenick ●

[Berlin]

interfered with. The Western sectors of Berlin could be over-run and occupied by the Red Army 'within an hour', as Kruschev is reported to have remarked to an American journalist early in 1961. (He apparently added, somewhat disingenuously, that he did not want Berlin and could not see why the Americans were so interested in it.)

Nevertheless, in spite of the weakness of our military posture, the fact remains that the allied forces are adequate as a 'tripwire'. Why? Because Berlin is not a military question at all but one of the hottest political potatoes in the world; and for all his threats and tough actions Kruschev recognises this. Militarily, Berlin is his. But for weighty political and strategic reasons he dare not seize it. This means that on the allied side the political and strategic campaign must be carried on with the greatest skill both in Berlin and wherever decisions affecting Berlin are discussed and taken. It is my settled conviction, based on my year in Berlin, that the Western position could be materially improved by a more realistic and up-to-date approach.

At the moment we have to negotiate from a weak position; and this is not good enough on such an important matter. Berlin is of the highest importance, because it has already nearly led to war and could well do so again. The Russians, both at Geneva in 1959 and since, have made it clear that they are open to an arrangement which would be reasonable from the point of view of the West. But the West have carried on with an old-fashioned type of diplomatic bargaining which may have seemed to hold the position but has in fact put us in an increasingly bad posture in Berlin. Not only are we, manifestly, on the defensive there to a degree that increases every day, and can be increased at the whim of the communist opposition, but we are also constantly made to look undignified and ineffectual.

To put it bluntly: if the West loses Berlin, NATO will collapse, which would be an even greater advance for the communists than their seizure of China. I am convinced that we shall lose this contest unless we alter our present methods. That, for me, is the lesson of my year's mission in Berlin— the last, as it happened, of my career as a diplomat.

Chapter 4

THE WALL GOES UP

July 1961 in Berlin I remember as being hot, heavy, humid. The more fortunate Berliners left the city for their holidays; others disported themselves on the Havel and in the Grunewald. The two magnificent Olympic swimming pools at the British Headquarters were much in use.

But all the time the flood of refugees from Eastern Germany, which had begun at the end of the war as soon as Germany was divided, was mounting, causing problems not just of an administrative but also of a political nature. Since the war three million had come across the divide, the speed varying considerably over the years. After Stalin's death in 1953 there was a sudden spurt owing to a burst of wishful thinking that a general relaxation was on the way, leading perhaps before long to the reunification of Germany. The pace then slackened; but after Kruschev's ultimatum of 1958 it quickened again from fear of the consequences of a separate Soviet-East German peace treaty. Throughout 1960 and 1961 the pace had been high, rising to a panic rate after Kruschev expressed to President Kennedy his determination to sign a peace treaty before the end of the

telligence does not claim to be soothsaying; no one
ve foretold Ulbricht's action until it had been
and this decision was probably not taken more than
f days or so before August 13.

onse to this critical development, what could or
Western allies have done? The first thing to do
ort these events by short immediate telegram to the
ffice, Bonn, Washington, Paris and Moscow. (An
which I used on another critical occasion was a
call to the Ambassador in Bonn. The service
he GDR was quick and efficient and I hope they
stening in to what was said.)

d troops were put on full alert, and then the Kom-
met at 10 a.m. with the US Commandant, Major-
atson, in the chair. We discussed possible counter-
both local and further afield. The Americans would
to put on a show of force; but we and the French
whether this would improve matters, with large
es at the ready all around Berlin. I suggested that,
saw Pact countries had announced their support of
ermans' action, reprisals might be taken again them
tionals; and it was agreed to refer this idea to our
ts. Nothing came of it so far as I know. Brandt
by invitation about an hour later, with Amrehn
colleagues. He was grave but statesmanlike. He
nded any rash action from the protecting powers
hed us for lack of firmness, though some of his col-
r tried to make scapegoats of us. In reply to some
f bad Allied Intelligence which a Christian Demo-
man made I did not hesitate to express my surprise
rlin Government's own information had not been
these disagreements came later and were never
August 13 we were all concerned together to

There was absolutely no s
East Berliners to the West
doubt many of us had cheri
for it is characteristic of t
easily led and as easily re
in the particular circumstar
succeeding months they w
reason. For we soon learn
Soviet forces in East Ger
Berlin, ready to act if req
efficiency of the action take
police, and the lack of an
allies, these forces were not
by the East German autho
incarcerating their fellow E
concentration camp, were
in check.

Looking back with hind
ligence was not too good
years back had greatly
hard knock as a result of t
the double agent, which h
doubt our allies' intellige
by his skilled treachery.
the West Berliners' own in
with families divided be
and more than the usual
the city, one might have
of Ulbricht's intentions.
materials had to be got r
number of East Germans

course in
could ha
decided;
a couple

In resp
should th
was to re
Foreign (
alternativ
telephone
through t
enjoyed li

All alli
mandatur
General V
measures,
have liked
questioned
Soviet for
as the Wa
the East (
or their na
governmen
joined us
and other
never dem
nor reproa
leagues lat
criticisms
crat spoke
that the B
better. Bu
serious. O

year. In July refugees were streaming over the border in all
shapes and sizes, young and old. On the whole they did not
look badly fed, unhealthy or particularly shabby. The
majority of them had left not for economic reasons but
because they found life in their police state intolerable and
expected it to get worse. The queues at the Marienfelde
reception and interrogation centre, to which they were direc-
ted, became longer and longer. From a hundred or two a day
the numbers rose until as the middle of August approached
the figure was nearly a couple of thousand. They were voting
with their feet.

As it happened, during this first month of my mission it
was the British turn to preside at meetings of the Allied Kommandatura. Jumbo Delacombe did so, while I presided at
meetings of the Deputy Commandants. Immediately, I was
introduced to its cumbersome procedure and got to know the
members of the bewildering variety of its tripartite sub-
committees—legal, social, economic and so on. In collaboration with the Governing Mayor, Willy Brandt, his deputy
Mayor Amrehn and the Government of Berlin we coped as
best we could with this problem of the refugees. At the very
end of July the allied Commandants and Ministers had a
discussion with Brandt, and all agreed that the communists
simply could not afford to let the flow of refugees continue to
increase, for reasons not only of prestige but of economics.
They were imposing new checks and controls every day but
to no avail. We expected something drastic and Brandt
thought that when it came there might well be a mass
outbreak from East to West Berlin of anything from 50,000
to 200,000 people. But none of us realised what cruel and
far-reaching measures were in store.

At about 2 a.m. in the very early morning of Sunday,
August 13, 1961, the communists went into action. The

guards already stationed at the dividing line between
the three Western sectors and the Soviet sector were
heavily reinforced with armed men of the East German Army
and the innumerable varieties of East German police. Large
numbers of workers were rushed up to put masses of barbed
wire fortifications in place; and behind this line building
materials for a wall were rapidly assembled. The inhabitants
of Berlin, including my family and myself, woke up that
Sunday to a radically new situation.

The East Berlin morning papers that day were full of
pompous announcements to the effect that this action had
been forced on the East German authorities by the aggressive, subversive, reactionary elements in West Berlin and
Bonn. The Warsaw Pact countries were said to have been
consulted, and to have given their full agreement. It seems
more than probable that when, earlier that month, Walter
Ulbricht, the well-hated but very efficient communist boss of
the GDR, had gone to Moscow to see his master Kruschev he
had told him that he had had enough of the refugee outflow
and must stop it whatever the consequences. Kruschev would
almost certainly have argued that a concrete division of
Berlin would have lamentable prestige and propaganda
results, not just for the GDR but for the whole communist
world. In spite of this, Kruschev must have finally con-
ceded Ulbricht's point as the daily flow mounted to a couple
of thousand : and a few days before August 13, Ulbricht,
resolute in his policy, had returned to Berlin. His Government now stated that adequate crossing points between the
East and West sectors would be held open, under East German control; but very few people felt inclined to test the truth
of this except the intrepid Western military police who went
through and back without hindrance. What in fact had
happened was that the existing eighty-eight crossing points

were at a blow cut down to twelve, and shortly after to seven; and these were all very strictly controlled.

There was absolutely no sign of the large-scale outbreak of East Berliners to the West which had been expected. No doubt many of us had cherished a few illusions on this score, for it is characteristic of the German people that they are easily led and as easily repressed. But it seems likely that in the particular circumstances of August 13, 1961, and the succeeding months they were half stunned, and with good reason. For we soon learnt that a large proportion of the Soviet forces in East Germany were concentrated around Berlin, ready to act if required. Owing to the rapidity and efficiency of the action taken by the East German forces and police, and the lack of any strong reaction by the Western allies, these forces were not called upon. The measures taken by the East German authorities, primarily for the purpose of incarcerating their fellow East Germans in Ulbricht's gigantic concentration camp, were sufficient to keep the population in check.

Looking back with hindsight it is now clear that our intelligence was not too good. British intelligence, which a few years back had greatly flourished in Berlin, had taken a hard knock as a result of the activities there of George Blake, the double agent, which had only recently been exposed. No doubt our allies' intelligence was affected to some extent too by his skilled treachery. But what is more surprising is that the West Berliners' own information was not more complete : with families divided between the West and East sectors, and more than the usual supply of agents and informers in the city, one might have expected someone to have got wind of Ulbricht's intentions. After all, a considerable quantity of materials had to be got ready and orders sent out to a large number of East Germans to prepare for the operation. But of course intelligence does not claim to be soothsaying; no one could have foretold Ulbricht's action until it had been decided; and this decision was probably not taken more than a couple of days or so before August 13.

In response to this critical development, what could or should the Western allies have done? The first thing to do was to report these events by short immediate telegram to the Foreign Office, Bonn, Washington, Paris and Moscow. (An alternative which I used on another critical occasion was a telephone call to the Ambassador in Bonn. The service through the GDR was quick and efficient and I hope they enjoyed listening in to what was said.)

All allied troops were put on full alert, and then the Kommandatura met at 10 a.m. with the US Commandant, Major-General Watson, in the chair. We discussed possible countermeasures, both local and further afield. The Americans would have liked to put on a show of force; but we and the French questioned whether this would improve matters, with large Soviet forces at the ready all around Berlin. I suggested that, as the Warsaw Pact countries had announced their support of the East Germans' action, reprisals might be taken again them or their nationals; and it was agreed to refer this idea to our governments. Nothing came of it so far as I know. Brandt joined us by invitation about an hour later, with Amrehn and other colleagues. He was grave but statesmanlike. He never demanded any rash action from the protecting powers nor reproached us for lack of firmness, though some of his colleagues later tried to make scapegoats of us. In reply to some criticisms of bad Allied Intelligence which a Christian Democrat spokesman made I did not hesitate to express my surprise that the Berlin Government's own information had not been better. But these disagreements came later and were never serious. On August 13 we were all concerned together to

devise the best measures we could against the communist outrage which it was clear to us might have incalculable consequences. Far away in their capitals officials and politicians
began to think. In Berlin the first reaction was to call a
committee meeting, which was hardly calculated to terrify the
enemy. Our troops there, all 10,000 of them, were put on the
alert. We decided on a protest to our Soviet 'colleague' in
East Berlin and recommended a further protest by the Western
governments to the Soviet Government. Good paper stuff.
After Willy Brandt had arrived to join our deliberations, we
went on discussing for hours what effective practical counter-
action we could launch. The fact is, we were all of us stupe-
fied, and almost as much taken by surprise as everyone else.
We decided to meet again early next day; and a French diplomat's suggestion that a quarter to eleven would be early enough
was overruled. So August 13 ended after more than the usual
quota of telegrams had been sent off to distant capitals asking
for instructions. On the next day the normal protests were
delivered, with the normal lack of effect. Berliners, on both
sides of the incipient wall, were baffled.

If General Clay had been in Berlin I have little doubt that
the tanks would have rolled that day. And this course of
action was discussed at length at our meeting. But we decided
against it and I do not believe that it would have done any
lasting good, even though it might have boosted the Berliners'
morale for a time. For though there was no actual wall
to knock down that first day, we should have had to mow
down ranks of scruffy-looking but quite well-armed East Germans, and their barbed wire. Whether the East Berlin population had then risen or not the Russians could not possibly

have allowed us to occupy their sector of Berlin. Their powerful forces, very much at the ready, would have gone into
action. There would then have ensued at best a battle, in
which the Western garrisons were bound to be defeated and
forced to retreat to their sectors; at worst, a war.

But although we did not find it easy to devise an effective
riposte to Ulbricht's outrage, this is not to say that we were
powerless. For my part, it occurred to me that we had in the
British sector the Soviet war memorial, guarded always by
Russian soldiers and regarded by them as sacred. I suggested
that we should surround the memorial with barbed wire,
inside which the Soviet guards might parade like animals in
a cage, and station a small British contingent nearby. All this
would be done, of course, in order to protect the interests of
our Soviet ally. Jumbo warmly welcomed my little scheme
and we put it into effect without delay. Very early one morning a Soviet colonel came through the Brandenburg Gate,
which had been walled off by the communists and which is
close by the memorial, and confronted our Chief of Military
Police, Colonel Dickie Richards, one of the best men we had
in Berlin. Quivering with rage, he asked what the hell we
were doing to his memorial. Dickie replied suavely that we
wanted to ensure the safety and properly respectful treatment
of the memorial and its guard against those who might wish
to molest them. The Soviet colonel said it was an outrage; no
such measures should have been taken without consultation
with the Soviet authorities. Dickie, gesturing at the Brandenburg Gate in its new condition, said that the Soviet authorities
seemed to be taking quite a lot of action themselves without
overmuch consultation. The colonel departed, apparently
heading for a coronary. This ploy proved a useful sanction on
several occasions in bringing the Russians to heel when their
provocations tended to go too far. They take very seriously the

right they have acquired by custom to send in guards every day; and it is within our power to stop them or to impose conditions on their access, whenever we like. Measures of this kind appeal to the Berliners and are all the more effective for being public. Without them I am sure the Soviet memorial would have been desecrated before now; and the Soviet authorities must be well aware of this.

A counter-measure of a different kind was initiated by Willy Brandt who at once appealed to President Kennedy for some tangible evidence of support, and the President responded by sending a very high-powered delegation to Berlin, led by his Vice-President, Lyndon Johnson. The delegation included General Lucius D. Clay (the former Military Governor who was still remembered as the saviour of the city in 1949 when the allied airlift beat the blockade), and 'Chip' Bohlen, probably the most able American diplomat, now Ambassador in Paris. They arrived on August 19 and were formally greeted at the Schöneberger Rathaus, the large building that houses the mayoral offices, the Senate and the House of Representatives of West Berlin. The Schöneberger Platz, as seen that afternoon from the terrace of the Rathaus, was packed with Berliners and they spread down the nearby streets as far as the eye could see. Some half a million people were present out of West Berlin's population of two and a quarter million. They had swarmed round the Vice-President's and General Clay's cars all the way from Tempelhof airfield and had now come to hear what these personal emissaries of President Kennedy had to say. Vice-President Johnson made a speech of little distinction, but he conveyed the President's pledge that the United States would defend the rights of Berlin with every means in her power. The vast crowd was in that emotional mood when it would cheer every mention of 'freedom' and 'independence' and all the clichés of public speech. When General Clay came to speak they nearly went berserk. Here was the man who had saved Berlin over ten years before, come back again to help save its people from an even graver threat to their freedom. They remembered; and they would not disperse for many hours.

Chapter 5

THE ALLIES REACT

By the end of August the Wall was a crude fact of life for Berliners. And although it has been described on countless occasions, no description, written, spoken or pictorial, has ever really brought home its utter repulsiveness. You have to imagine a wall being put up, under the supervision of heavily armed, trigger-happy Teddy boys, all along Whitehall, across the middle of Trafalgar Square, up Charing Cross Road and Tottenham Court Road and far beyond for well over twenty miles, northwards and southwards, its arbitrary line ruthlessly cutting off people, buildings, traffic, business. There are half a dozen gaps, each heavily defended by road blocks and armed thugs. Foreigners are allowed through one, people from West London through another, Middlesex men through another, and so on. It is worse than that in Berlin, because if you are allowed through into the Eastern sector you find there a wretched wilderness of a part-city, where your friends and relations go in fear of the police. To cap it all, the Wall is not even a particularly substantial erection : it is unimpressive, badly built, thoroughly squalid, what I described at the time as 'tank bait', so tempting was it to nudge it down. I had

seen the wall that divides Jerusalem, and there is something
specially shameful about that : one of the holy cities of the
world cut through the middle so that some of the shrines are
in Jordan and some in Israel. But, in the materialistic world
of today, that wall lacks the explosive danger of the Berlin
Wall. It is not part of a wall of iron girdling the whole world.

The immediate effect of the building of the Wall on everyone in Berlin was that of a powerful blow on the head.
Reactions were slow : the springs of action were numbed. The
daily livelihood of some 200,000 East Berliners—the *Grenz-
gänger* who came to work in West Berlin and their families—
was cut off completely. Yet we never heard of any serious
protest from them, let alone any action against the fellow-
citizens who were oppressing them. Some were found work,
of a far less profitable kind, in East Berlin; many were ruthlessly moved to more or less distant parts of the GDR. Other
East Berliners who were unfortunate enough to live on, or too
near, the line of the Wall or the West Berlin-GDR frontier
were also removed lock, stock and barrel, and where their
houses were judged to be in the way they were knocked down.
The number of East Berliners whom their own authorities
have allowed into West Berlin since August 1961 has been
very small. The railwaymen, needed to operate the railway
through the city, form the largest group. They travel freely
in and through West Berlin. After them come those coura-
geous people who dare everything in order to escape. Many
hundreds have got through. Scores have lost their lives in the
attempt.

The West Berliners were equally stunned at first. The Wall
did not affect their livelihood to anything like the same
extent; but it soon became apparent that the East German

authorities would only allow a very few, carefully vetted, West Berliners through, and this has remained the position. So families were divided, friends cut off from friends. Those pathetic pictures of people waving to each other across the Wall are no mere propaganda; this was the only way mother could establish contact with son, or brother with brother. The strain proved too much for some West Berliners and there was an exodus from the city. This never reached significant proportions, and it lasted only a short time. A high proportion of those leaving came from the richer classes, though even these mostly kept on their houses in Berlin and returned from time to time. But as Berlin has few rich residents and no 'society' this movement was not important. The solid Berlin citizens, whose modest capital consisted in their houses, plots, business and skills, stayed put. Trade recovered in a few months. So did morale. Economic inducements brought businesses and workers from West Germany, and beyond, to Berlin. General Clay threw in his great influence to persuade some American companies to invest in the city. So the crisis was surmounted. But the fact must be faced : Berlin's population is numerically static and ageing.

From time to time, as was only natural, the wrath of the West Berliners boiled over. When the East Berlin authorities had the impertinence to demand that the allies should clear a strip of 100 metres all along their own side of the Wall in order to contribute to the general safety we were in no mood to comply and they were curtly told to mind their own business. The Vopos (*Volkspolizei*) were stoned and jeered at. On a few occasions small bombs blew holes in the Wall. The Western allies had to handle these situations with great care since protests of this kind did little good but merely gave the Vopos an excuse for violent retaliation. Particularly tempting targets for demonstrators are the series of motor cars in which the Soviet war memorial guard and members of BASC go daily to and from their work in West Berlin. Many of these incidents were undoubtedly fomented by *agents provocateurs*.

Willy Brandt and his Government in West Berlin have adopted an admirable attitude to the Wall throughout. He and his colleagues have lost no opportunity of pounding home the nauseating character of the Wall, describing it as a concrete demonstration of Ulbricht's failure to convince his people of the joys of life in East Germany. They have taken measures to attract visitors from all over the world, ranging from Heads of State to ordinary tourists, to come and see for themselves. Not even Berlin's famous night-clubs, or 'My Fair Lady' which has been enjoying a run similar to that in London, will outlast the Wall in the memories of visitors to Berlin. Indeed, I only know of one person who has been to Berlin and not seen the Wall.

Brandt has also worked patiently away to arrange small, gradual relaxations on the restrictions on East and West Berliners. He has not had much success so far, and the hopes —always rather unreasonable—that the East Germans would allow large-scale relaxations at each of the two Christmasses since the Wall went up have been dashed. Nevertheless his method is right, and one day, when the general East-West atmosphere is less frigid, I think it will bring results. His former deputy Amrehn's method of repeatedly demanding in his speeches that 'the Wall must come down' will never have any effect.

Passage through the Wall, at the crossing points designated by the East Germans, presents no special difficulty to people from anywhere outside Berlin, including West Germans. Occasionally there are annoyances over passports, but normally the flow is unhindered. In my view as many people as possible should go to Berlin, particularly those from non-aligned countries who believe the Cold War is a Western fiction. They should take a good look at the Wall, approaching it from the beautifully laid out roads and buildings of West Berlin. Then they should go through the Vopo-guarded hole in the Wall and look equally long at the Eastern sector. We found nobody remained 'non-aligned' in Berlin.

The Wall is not even popular with East Germany's allies and friends. No fanfares greeted it from the satellite countries. From Krushchev downwards they have all been embarrassed about it. Kruschev, when questioned, has always given brief, evasive answers. It is seldom mentioned as such by the communists. It becomes, euphemistically, 'one of the measures forced on the GDR Government by the aggressive imperialists'.

As for the Western allies, we have generally followed the line of condemning the Wall and all it stands for on every suitable occasion, while refraining from violent action against it. I think this is right. The Americans have wanted to teach the communists a lesson by pushing a bit of it down or putting troops through a crossing-point into the Eastern sector; and in October 1961 they briefly did this. But the Russians could not possibly allow us to do this on any large scale or for any length of time. Consequently, little would be achieved beyond a temporary boost to morale; and the probability is that the East Germans would take it out on the Berliners in some form.

The Wall is a brutal and uncivilised thing. It causes great human suffering. You cannot leave West Berlin without running into it or the equally horrible death strip round the Western sectors. Its existence preys on many people. But the Berliners and their allies have proved that, as they must live with it, they will not let it break their morale. Berlin remains the greatest German industrial city, and the Wall has not affected that. The communists hope that thanks to the Wall

West Berlin will 'wither on the bough'. There is no sign of that so far, and I remain confident that the West Berliners will carry on with the cheerfulness they have shown throughout all their tribulations.

One result of the Wall, unsavoury object though it is, has been to allow the communists to relax over Berlin and not to insist on their ultimata being met. The Wall has in fact served to stabilise a situation which was getting dangerously fluid. Ulbricht has even been able to turn more attention to improving the economic situation of the GDR.

So long, therefore, as West Berlin morale remains good, and with it West Berlin productivity, her inhabitants can continue to lead good, happy and profitable lives in spite of the Wall. There is a dangerous and insidious argument, encouraged of course by the communists, that Berlin can never pull through because she is an artificial city. Certainly, her situation is artificial both geographically and politically owing to the results of the two German wars and the blunders of allied policy. The *va-et-vient* in the streets and shops has not the liveliness of that in true capitals situated in the heart of their countries. But there is no doubt that she can continue to flourish as she does at present; and that it is vital to the West that she should do so. Meanwhile, it is essential that the West should take advantage of the communists' more relaxed line on Berlin to reach a better political agreement than the occupation statutes provide. Such an agreement would hold out hope for the whole of Berlin and the ultimate removal of the Wall of Shame.

One of the most powerful aids to the West Berliners' morale in the early days was the visit of the American Vice-President, Lyndon Johnson, and his party. The announcement soon afterwards that General Clay would come back to Berlin as President Kennedy's special representative continued the process; and his arrival in September and the immediate deployment of his boundless energy gave it a further powerful boost. For the next couple of months steps were taken on both sides to strengthen their positions and it became clear that a yet more serious crisis was bound to come. The communists were increasing the strength and beastliness not only of the Wall but of the ring of deadly obstructions all round the perimeter of the Western sectors. The allies, though owing to their cumbersome administrative machinery they were seldom able to take the initiative, hit back hard wherever possible; and an additional United States battle group was brought into the city. Meanwhile President Kennedy mobilised a great many troops and sent considerable extra forces to Europe. He stated in terms that the United States would in the last resort fight for Berlin, and there is no doubt that the American people were behind him. Discussions between the Americans, British, French and Germans on Berlin policy began in Washington and also less intensively in NATO. Broadly, it was the Americans who were always firm, and occasionally even rash; but equally it was they who saved the day. The British agreed with many of their firm proposals, but took little action to back them. The French approach was cynical and *dégagé*: but they contributed much good sense to the discussions. The Federal German Government were out consistently to exploit the situation for their own ends, and it is not surprising that they fell foul of the United States more than once in the process. On the other side, Kruschev breathed fire and slaughter in the background, seconded by his henchman Ulbricht: another exhibition of the hatred of German for German which is surely one of the most atrocious phenomena of our age.

There is no doubt that the successful perpetration of the Wall—and the lack of any effective reaction from the West—had made the East Germans cock-a-hoop, and they began to indulge in everything from pinpricks like tossing tear gas bombs over the Wall to the most brutal outrages against their fellow-citizens who tried to escape to freedom. General Clay, who had lost no time in making his influence felt, decided that it was time to give them a jolt. The opportunity for action occurred one Saturday evening in October when my American opposite number, Allen Lightner, drove with a party in his private car to the crossing at Friedrichstrasse—Checkpoint Charlie—in order to go to the opera in East Berlin. He and his party were stopped and asked to show their passes. Sticking to the line always followed by the Americans he explained who he and his friends were and politely refused to comply. Thereupon the East German officials declined to let him through the road block. He demanded to see a Soviet officer, but received no satisfaction. A detachment of the US Army then formed up, with arms at the port, and escorted him in his car a short way into the Eastern sector : honour being thus satisfied, and the opera nearly over anyway, they then escorted him back. The Americans had made a token incursion into the Soviet sector of Berlin.

The communists made no strong reaction but continued their harassing tactics, refusing admission to American officials, even when in official cars and on business, unless they agreed to show their passes. This was General Clay's opportunity for a showdown. He reckoned two things : that the Russians were not prepared to go to war over incidents in Berlin, and that it would be a good move to smoke them out and expose the futility of the official Soviet line, which was that they were powerless in East Berlin because it was the capital of the independent GDR. General Clay was right. He installed himself in the American operations room near Friedrichstrasse, got into direct communication with the White House and the State Department and ordered the

American tanks to roll right up to the road blocks. The Russians were forced to respond. Up to now they had never appeared in force anywhere near the Wall. Now they whistled up their tanks and took up positions directly opposite the Americans, a few yards away. Since some of the Russian tanks had come from behind the Brandenburg Gate opposite the British sector, we took action in support of the Americans by moving up both tanks and anti-tank guns. A few hours later the Americans withdrew their tanks a short distance : whereupon the Russians followed suit. Later the Americans moved up again; again the Soviet tanks appeared. This test of resolution continued for two or three tense days. Then, with the American tanks still at the road blocks, the Soviet tanks finally withdrew. They had chickened.

The Americans, who had made their point with force, were criticised by some fainthearts for playing an unnecessarily dangerous game. They were also criticised for not consulting their allies in advance. My view, which I expressed to General Al Watson, was that it was a successful operation, well executed if a little dangerous, and that they had kept us pretty well informed considering its warlike nature and the consequent need for all speed and secrecy. The West Berliners were delighted to see the initiative taken, for once, by the West, and regarded the whole affair as a salutary thwack in the teeth for the communists. At the same time they were, naturally, a bit nervous that serious shooting might break out; and some rather cynically questioned what lasting results were obtained by simply moving the tanks forwards and backwards. I maintain my view that the basic calculation behind it was correct. Provided the allies fully supported initiatives of this kind by the Americans, a strengthening of our joint position should result in the future. But for various reasons we were to be disappointed in this expectation.

This incident showed General Clay back in his old form. He could recall the days when, as Military Governor of Berlin, he had had a most effective collaboration with our own Governor, General Sir Brian (now Lord) Robertson. Those were the days of the airlift when what Clay said went. Now he was sixty-five but still extremely fit and whippy. His energy and drive were terrific; and he had little patience with the somewhat cumbrous officialdom of the Kommandatura. He had volunteered to come from his highly paid job with Continental Canning Inc; and though his coming was bound to put some noses out of joint, for he ranked in the American hierarchy only just below the United States Ambassador in Bonn, I myself liked and admired him and his straightforward character.

In the eight months he spent in the city he did a job for the morale of the Berliners which no one else could have done. I have little doubt that Clay would have liked to direct all allied policy as a 'supremo'; but he met with opposition from the French and British Governments. His relations with Jumbo slipped badly as a result of an incident at a dinner party given for him and his guest, Lord Robertson, soon after the tanks had rolled in October. Clay stated that the British had done nothing to help on this occasion. This was not correct, as we had moved our tanks and anti-tank guns uptown to the Brandenburg Gate in support. Jumbo pointed this out with rather excessive heat for a host, particularly as several other guests including Steel, were listening with bated breath; and the evening was not a success. We were horrified to learn later that the story had got around Bonn.

Two months later another clash occurred in Berlin between the Americans and the communists which could have had more serious consequences. One day a State Department official set out in his official car on an official mission to see the Soviet

Commandant. The East Germans had been officially warned in advance. In fact, the whole thing could not have been more official. At the checkpoint the American was asked to show his identity card; this, in accordance with custom, he declined to do, and he returned to base without delivering his message. A few days later General Watson, the US Commandant, set out on a similar errand accompanied by the same State Department official. This unfortunate man was asked again to identify himself, although no commandant's car had ever been stopped before. He refused and after some argle-bargle Al Watson decided to turn back and leave *his* mission uncompleted. He then retaliated by denying the Soviet Commandant and his political adviser, who called himself a lieutenant-colonel, access to the US sector. In effect, as East German regulations stipulated that the Russians must use only the Friedrichstrasse crossing, this meant that unless they broke the rules of their 'sovereign independent' friends their two leading representatives were excluded from all three Western sectors. In order to enforce this ban the American troops at Checkpoint Charlie were ordered to produce a couple of photographs to any Soviet vehicle conveying a colonel, and to ask the inmates: 'Are you Colonel Soloviev, that's this one, or Lieutenant-Colonel Alexeieff, that one?' This device, since it disrupted the agreement governing military personnel and vehicles, could be regarded as either heavy-handed, farcical or dangerous. Once again I let Al Watson know that in my view he was fully justified in taking these reprisals which the communists well understood. This time the communists did not immediately react. I heard Soloviev grumble that his photograph was being bandied about as if it were that of a wanted criminal; and he later tweaked the Americans' tail by entering the Western sectors once or twice by an 'illegal' crossing point. In due course he retaliated by banning the US Commandant from the Soviet sector. But the truth was that there was very little point anyway in personal contact between the American and Soviet Commandants, as they were both ready to admit.

I personally favoured improved contacts with the Russians, not from any facile optimism but simply to probe their intentions. But the futility of the formal contacts between commandants had led to the conclusion—mistaken in my view—that even informal contacts could have no value. The only places where we met them regularly were in Spandau gaol and in the Berlin Air Safety Centre. The gaol meetings proved useful once or twice for passing messages on current difficulties, and the BASC was effective for exchanging information about Western and communist flight plans. I would have liked to go a bit further. I always agreed that members of my staff should discuss any matters which their Soviet opposite numbers cared to raise, and sometimes this led to business getting done.

The Russians maintain a large Embassy in East Berlin which was headed in my time by Mr Pervukhin, a former member of the Politburo now somewhat *dégringolé*. Technically we did not recognise it as an Embassy since it was accredited to a non-existent government. However, when the Soviet number two telephoned one day to ask whether he might call on me I agreed without any hesitation. This caused some consternation amongst our allies. In the event he got one of those Soviet diplomatic headaches and could not come. I later made an appointment to see Pervukhin, immediately after seeing Commandant Soloviev and drinking some cheerful glasses of vodka with him. By an extraordinary coincidence Pervukhin was 'called away' just before my appointment to a meeting with the GDR Government and I was fobbed off with his Minister. We had an hour's talking and drinking that was not entirely a waste of time. Some time after the

Wall, members of the Soviet Embassy began coming to West Berlin on 'cultural' errands, and we kept a sharp eye on this. We also watched the Head of the Czechoslovak Military Mission, who was really a history professor and was allowed to live and work in the British sector and even to be a member of the British Officers' Club : a facility which I deplored.

This question of crossing from the Eastern sector to the West and vice versa kept cropping up. The press used to exaggerate the small divergencies of practice followed by the allies, which were not intrinsically important but were easily exploited by the communists. As far as military vehicles, military personnel in uniform and ordinary civilians were concerned the allied procedures were the same. Military vehicles and uniformed personnel showed no sort of pass, and were let through by the East Berlin authorities without hindrance. Ordinary civilians of every nationality, excluding only government servants, submitted to ordinary passport and customs checks. It was only in the case of government officials that there was any divergence of practice, and this dated from long before the Wall. The British considered it reasonable that an official should show, on demand, a document proving him to be what he claimed to be, but we never allowed the communists to handle it in any way. This always worked well. The Americans and the French, however, refused to allow their officials to show anything at all to the East Berlin authorities. When this refusal led them into trouble the American Minister told me he only wished they had adopted our sensible practice long before, but they could not do so now as it would look like a climb-down.

Of course, the whole trouble was utterly futile, as was the Soviet parrot-cry that the GDR were 'sovereign' in their sector; and I was able once to demonstrate this. I was going in my official car to see the Soviet Commandant and word of my

intention had been sent to the East German checkpoint. I
thought we would try to get through without the usual showing of passes. At the checkpoint my interpreter told the *Vopo*
(the policeman on guard) who I was; and to my satisfaction
we swept through the barrier unchecked. I mentioned this to
Colonel Soloviev as an example of what could be done if
people tried hard enough, but although he was in an exceedingly hospitable mood that morning—Jumbo and I had to
swallow half a dozen vodkas apiece before we got away, and
even then had to refuse a bottle of champagne—he muttered
something about inefficiency. When going out at the checkpoint I tried on my little ruse again; the *Vopo* insisted, almost
pleaded, that I should just hold up my pass for him to see. He
had received his master's orders.

Chapter 6

THE POLITICAL BACKGROUND

Berlin has become one of the most constant, pressing subjects in the dialogue between the USA and the USSR, or, more exactly, between President Kennedy and Mr Kruschev. When Kruschev delivered his 'ultimatum' in 1958, to the effect that he intended to sign a treaty with the GDR within six months which would abolish all the Western allies' rights in Berlin, the upshot was a long meeting in Geneva some months later in which the US representatives took the lead as *primi inter pares*.

Kruschev began to rumble again about his treaty late in 1960. But he tested the newly installed President first on two other fronts: Laos and Cuba. On Laos, *pace* Lord Home, he would never have allowed world war to occur. On Cuba, first round, he had only to sit back and watch the American fiasco.

The new Berlin crisis began in earnest when Kennedy met Kruschev in Vienna in June 1961. Kruschev took a very tough line and repeated his ultimatum with all force and apparent sincerity. I am told that the President emerged from the discussion pale and shaken. Kruschev and Ulbricht followed this up with many aggressive repetitions of the theme that the Western allies could either join in the treaty and like it, or they could lump it. Kennedy withdrew to consider the best riposte.

I was at my post in Berlin from July 2, 1961, to June 2, 1962; and this coincided pretty well with the Clay epoch from September 1961 to May 1962. During all that time Berlin was in the headlines almost every day. Although it is not generally appreciated in Britain, the risk of nuclear war existed throughout the autumn of 1961 because Kennedy had concluded, rightly, that only by convincing Kruschev that he meant business could he choke him off rash action over Berlin. There were four specific crises which could have led to war. The first was the building of the Wall in August 1961. Then, after Clay's arrival in Berlin, there was the Friedrich-strasse confrontation of American and Soviet tanks in October. In December the *Vopo* stopped the US Commandant from crossing to see his Soviet opposite number and tempers flared. In January and February 1962 the Russians interfered with allied traffic in the air corridors. I describe these in detail eleswhere; here I want to give the political background against which each of these dangerous games was played.

The political interplay was constant and intricate, for great principles were liable to find themselves mixed up, at every level, with petty but significant matters of detail. After their Vienna meeting Kennedy saw that he must make it clear to Kruschev, if necessary by force, that the West would not yield over Berlin. He called hundreds of thousands of reservists to the colours and despatched large extra forces to Europe. He sent General Clay, the Berliners' idol, as his personal repre-sentative to Berlin with, at first, a pretty free hand. He told his Secretary of State, Dean Rusk, first to get the agreement of the British, French and Germans to US-Soviet conversations; and secondly to get these going, both personally and through Ambassador Llewellyn Thompson in Moscow.

The first of these tasks was difficult enough. The Americans had to make the running at every stage and at every level. It was not too difficult to argue on the broad principles : West Berlin must remain free, the Western forces must stay, free access must continue to be guaranteed by the Russians. But this obviously did not give much room for fruitful negotiation, and it was extremely difficult to get the allies to show enough confidence in the American negotiators.

The broad pattern was usually as follows. The Americans would put up some new idea or nuance. The British, after taking instructions from HMG, would agree that it might be tried out at a pinch, but would not guarantee to approve any follow-up action until the next step had been fully considered. The French either had no instructions; or they expressed disinterest in the whole manoeuvre; or they said 'non'. The West Germans usually expressed doubts whether this step would help German reunification, and suggested, instead, some much tougher line of a kind which would obviously bring the discussions to a standstill.

Rusk and Thompson soldiered on, greatly to their credit. Mr Gromyko and his colleagues may be no longer the 'nyet'-boys of the Molotov era, but they have a more effective and equally infuriating technique. Mr Christian Herter, then Secretary of State, complained that at Geneva in 1959 he had over fifty hours discussion with the Soviet representatives going over and over the same ground and hardly covering more than a few new inches by the end of it. This was the method followed by the Soviet representatives in 1961–62.

I am not sure whether the 1959 marathon record was beaten, but there was little in it. The American negotiators must often have felt tempted to give in to boredom or exasperation, but they did not. They applied another technique which the communists also use. The exact moods and nuances of expression used by the Soviet representative on the same topic on different occasions were painstakingly compared to see whether there was some small advance in approach, even when there was clearly none in substance. Once in January 1962 Dean Rusk told us that he thought the first signs of a thaw had been detected. I studied the telegrams as through a microscope. I could see nothing new. Thinking I must have missed something I asked Sir Christopher Steel in Bonn if he could throw any light : he could not. It appeared later that some detail had been slightly misinterpreted, and we were not really any further forward than before.

To my mind these discussions—the Germans objected to the use of the word negotiations—were a fine example of an art which is still of the highest importance, secret diplomacy. This term has fallen into disrepute : it might be better described as the confidential discussion of diplomatic business, which is just as important as for any other type of business. What is essential in such long-drawn-out discussions is that one should know one's own objectives; and, secondly, that one should keep an eye on the other side to make sure that they are not about to spring a nasty surprise—as at Pearl Harbour. In this particular exchange the Americans judged matters admirably. They did not go into the discussions with the hope of quick successes or even results of any kind, estimating rightly that the Russians also wanted to talk at length. In the end, they achieved two great successes. When there was a real danger of war they kept the 'jaw, jaw, jaw' going. And during and after these conversations extraneous influences, including Cuba round two, had so modified the international atmosphere that Kruschev was able to adopt the far more relaxed attitude which he now has on Berlin.

The British, I fear, are apt to be less good at this type of negotiation. Perhaps it is because we lack the ultimate force and hence the self-confidence: we operate more on the margin. Whatever the reason, the effect often seems to be that we prolong the talking without having a clear idea of our real objectives. This may help in the short term to preserve the *status quo*; but its weakness is that the other side are liable to call the bluff at a moment of their choosing.

Besides these discussions at the highest level, throughout this period more day-to-day matters were being thrashed out in all the capitals concerned, and particularly in the quadripartite 'Ambassadorial Group' in Washington.

If I may be allowed a flight of fancy, this is the sort of exchange which one might have found on one's desk in Berlin :

1. *Cypher telegram from Washington to Foreign Office. Repeated to Bonn, Paris, Berlin and Ulan Bator.*

No. 11,674 of Sept. 1. Reference Bonn tel. no. 1758 of Aug. 30. Following from Minister.

'American Under-Secretary of State called urgent meeting of Ambassadorial Group today to discuss Bonn report of Soviet Commandant's incursion into British sector. He said that US Embassy in Bonn had not yet reported, but assuming information was correct incident seemed very serious and counter-measures should be urgently considered. He proposed that schedule 1A should now be applied in entirety, and he would go so far as to support application of 1B if his colleagues thought this appropriate.

'I said that my instructions were not yet complete. In principle I thought I could support the application of 1A, but

I could go no further at present. I would let my colleagues know more as soon as I could.

'The French representative (a third secretary) apologised for the fact that all his superiors were too busy to come to this meeting. He had absolutely no instructions; but he would guess that if he received any they would be in the sense that he should play no part in the exercise. He wondered whether in fact a serious incident had taken place?

'The German representative said that he agreed that a firm reaction was called for but it must be taken in the right context. Nothing must be done to damage the prospects of German reunification or to encourage the Russians to exert further oppression on the German inhabitants of the Soviet Zone. (Here I omit 200 words on similar themes). He wondered whether we should not try in the first place to get unanimous NATO action.

'The Chairman summed up by saying that the matter clearly needed further reflection by all and he suggested a further meeting in a few days' time.

'This was generally approved.'

2. *Cypher telegram from Berlin to Bonn. Repeated to FO, No. 1503 of Sept. 1, Washington, Paris and Moscow, not, repeat, not to Ulan Bator. Ref. Washington tel. no. 11,674.*

'We are in the dark on this as we do not seem to have received your tel. under ref. Please forward.'

3. *Cypher telegram from Bonn to Berlin.*
No. 990 of Sept. 2. Ref. your tel. no. 1503.

'Regret that by an oversight you were not sent our earlier tel. Text follows.

'Usually reliable source reports that Soviet Commandant entered British sector on Thursday in a clandestine manner and through unusual crossing point. He was driven to deserted part near Gatow airfield where he got out and ran around suspiciously, armed with a curious weapon which source could not identify. This went on for some time. Source managed to glimpse him soon after he got into his car. He was breathing heavily and appeared overjoyed at what he had done. Car drove swiftly off and returned to Soviet sector.'

4. *Cypher tel. from Washington to FO, repeated to Bonn, Paris, Berlin and Moscow.*

'No. 12,444 of Sept. 2. Ref. my tel. no. 11674. For "Ulan Bator" read "Moscow".'

5. *Cypher tel. from Berlin to FO. Repeat Washington, Bonn, Paris, Moscow.*

'No. 1551 of Sept. 2. Ref. Bonn report on Soviet Comdt's incursion.

'You will be receiving our report in McD's letter to Smith of Aug. 31. Gist is as follows :

'Some time ago Soviet Commandant, who is keen butterfly fancier, told us that he had heard of presence of very rare butterfly in open fields of British sector on the way to Gatow. He would be most grateful if, at some time suitable to us, he might be allowed to come unobtrusively across for a little butterfly-hunting.

'Soloviev has been rather helpful on certain matters recently and we thought it right to agree. He only came at the time and by the route we indicated and frolicked about. We tailed him throughout.

'He has since written saying he caught two specimens which gave him enormous pleasure. He wants us to go and see them. Meanwhile he has sent us a couple of bottles of vodka. What is more important, there are distinct indications that he will agree to a settlement of the R. exclave problem practically on our terms.'

In fact, Soloviev, as he once told me, liked best of all not hunting butterflies but fishing through ice. But the point of this frivolous excursion is simply to show the way the powers concerned in Berlin used to behave. The Ambassadorial Group was nevertheless most useful in bringing together the views of the four governments on a wide range of subjects affecting Berlin. The fact that the Group could seldom reach agreement was the fault of its constituent members. I think it attempted to cover too wide a range. One day it would be discussing some trifling incident concerning passes in Berlin; the next it might be proposing to put forward to NATO a scheme for barring Soviet and satellite aircraft from the West or for imposing some types of economic sanctions if the emergency arose. It set up various sub-committees consisting of quite junior representatives who sometimes telegraphed all over the place at as great length as the Group itself. Since their views could not be in any way decisive this seemed a great waste of time and money. But, in spite of this, the Group proved a useful forum and helped governments to know each other's minds, if not always to make up their own.

NATO as such was only brought in to the Berlin problem in connection with economic or other measures which would be necessary if the situation were to deteriorate to the brink of war or simply to ensure that all the western allies knew what was afoot. This was done quite deliberately in order to remove any grounds from Kruschev's periodical accusation—which I do not think he makes very seriously—that West Berlin is a forward base of the aggressive NATO nations. Certainly the three Western allies with forces there regard it as nothing of the sort.

I must mention one committee which was set up in contact with NATO, but not under its aegis, and which functioned most efficiently. This was a small tripartite committee, whose job was to counter Soviet interference in the air corridors. On the basis of information sent with the utmost possible rapidity by the three Powers' representatives in Berlin—via US channels, as they were the most efficient—this committee worked out the appropriate counter-measures and arrangements for allied civilian and military air traffic in the corridors, and sent us back the necessary instructions. These always seemed to hit the right note : suitably tough if the Russians were being tiresome, but reasonably rearranging some schedule by a few minutes if that met the case. In very tricky cases General Norstad himself gave the decision. He did not hesitate on one occasion to countermand an order of General Clay's which he considered unnecessarily dangerous. Eventually the Russians called it off. By then more civilian passengers were flying to and from the city than when the interference began; and the Americans had had useful practice in flying into Tempelhof their gigantic Globemaster transports.

To complete this survey of the political background we must look further at London, Moscow and Bonn. We in Berlin always found the Foreign Office helpful in giving quick decisions when required, or approving those we had to take rapidly on the spot. It was rather different with the British Embassy in Bonn. They were seldom in a position to give a final decision; but we were in duty bound to keep them informed, and I think they were sometimes apt to make comments *pour se faire valoir*. But their business was to carry on relations with the Federal Government; and this was quite different from ours which was to run West Berlin in concert with the local government on the basis of the Occupation Statute. The answer, I am sure, is much greater independence for the Western representatives in Berlin; and this is an essential point in my suggested solution of the whole problem.

As for our Ambassador in Moscow, he had a somewhat

thankless task. Sir Frank Roberts is one of our very best men
and I am glad to see him now installed as Ambassador in
Bonn, where he will certainly get things moving. In Moscow
his role was apt to be reduced to that of a protest-conveyor,
since it was agreed by the allies that his US colleague should
do most of the hard bargaining, while it depends entirely on
Kruschev's whim whether important Soviet Government communication to HMG are made in Moscow or in London or
New York. But Frank Roberts and his staff always had their
ears to the ground and they did all that they possibly could.

The outstanding Western representative in Moscow at the
time was the Federal German Ambassador, Herr Kroll. This
roly-poly man got together with the similarly shaped Kruschev
on terms of personal friendship, and his mastery of the Russian
language helped a lot. He even got down to brass tacks in his
personal talks with Kruschev and probed some really forward-
looking ideas on Berlin. It is not surprising, perhaps, that he
was recalled in a hurry and kicked out. This was something of
an omen : it occurred during my time in Berlin, and I had
some sympathy with him.

Chapter 7

A DIPLOMAT'S LIFE IN BERLIN

I had got into the swing of my job as rapidly as I could. Some of the work consisted of the usual diplomatic chores; but not much, for Berlin was nothing like the usual run of diplomatic posts. Its problems, and the machinery devised to tackle them, were much too complex. In some ways my job was more like that of a governor than a diplomat. I had to give—or withold—my approval to all legislation proposed by the Berlin Senate. We kept a specially sharp eye on measures affecting the police; and partly as a result they developed into a first-class force, able to man the Wall with firm discipline. We also saw to it that they did not take on the role of a para-military unit. As another example, I had on my staff the Governor of Spandau gaol, where the remaining war criminals are incarcerated, and I had to discuss with him from time to time their welfare.

These are not the normal activities of a diplomat, and they gave rise to situations which required the exercise of judgment and initiative on the spot, backed, of course, by instructions from Government. Unfortunately, as I have now come to realise, there was more to it than that. Sandwiched between

me and the Foreign Office in London was my immediate
chief, Sir Christopher Steel, the British Ambassador in
Bonn.

I will not pretend that he and I would ever have become
bosom friends. Our temperaments were poles apart. Like
Jumbo Delacombe, he was in his last post before going into
retirement. He would come up to Berlin every five weeks or
so to supervise us and also to play a few rounds of golf—
though I am not entirely sure that this particular manifesta-
tion of British *sang-froid* made a direct appeal to the tough,
modern-minded leaders of Berlin. He had known Berlin in
different circumstances as he had served there twice before,
and he told me at the start that he had asked for me personally for this critical post. He appeared friendly to both
Elizabeth and myself and seemed to approve of my work. He
was always hospitable on my occasional visits to Bonn, just as
we were on his visits to Berlin.

I never liked going to Bonn, to that sleepy university town,
set in an unattractive part of the Rhine Valley in a heavy slug-
gish atmosphere, damp and depressing to the spirits; a sort of
foggy bottom. It was, of course, full of diplomatic missions,
which were a source of wild rumours and premature leaks and
intrigues at every level. When I arrived there I would be
greeted as if I were a poor relation up from the provinces.
The kind people of the capital were ready to extend to my
little problems an infinitely patient hearing. But though we
felt that Bonn was as distant from us and our problems as
Washington, we had to accept things as they were and make
the best of them. And so several times I made the journey across
the Soviet zone to visit the Ambassador in Bonn. I say Soviet
zone; but more usually it was known as the 'so-called GDR',
a disapproving description used by the allies on all official
occasions to emphasise their refusal to admit that it exists as

a state. It was an eerie experience, travelling down that *Autobahn*, for though the road was good enough and the countryside was beautiful, there seemed to be hardly any signs of life. I remember the French Ambassador, a precise, deceptively high-powered man, arriving late for a meeting in Berlin: he explained that while motoring through the so-called GDR his car had unfortunately collided with a so-called tree.

People forget the unique geographical position of Berlin, a Western exclave more than a hundred miles behind the Iron Curtain. They do not realise that although without any prospect of becoming viable economically on her own, bound always to be dependent on routes of access to the West, and although the communists have made continual efforts to strangle her, Berlin, or rather West Berlin, is now the greatest German industrial city. Even to residents it constantly comes as a surprise to find it so spread-out: it covers in all about four hundred and fifty square miles, of which the Western sectors amount to rather over half. The Wall itself is twenty-eight miles long, the perimeter of the Western sectors about seventy miles and that of the Eastern sector only slightly less. The British sector is conveniently placed in the middle; but for the French to visit the Americans entails quite a trek. It was nothing for me to motor thirty or forty miles in a day about my business.

The actual boundaries are full of anomalies. There was a small tongue of land attached to the British sector only by a narrow track running through communist territory. It contained a couple of poor farms and a few additional acres; and the communists thought they could strangle it by cutting the access route. So we sent a detachment of soldiers to camp there and patrol the track: they also guarded the solitary schoolboy living there on his way to and from school. The communists soon laid off. Another anomaly was in the village

of Staaken, where the line between the Eastern zone and the
British sector ran down the middle of the village high street.
The Communists built up the usual death-strip beginning
with barbed wire on their edge of the road, but they left their
half of the road temptingly unwired in the hope than an un-
wary West Berliner might step across this unmarked 'frontier'
and be fair game for the *Vopo*'s guns. We had to mark a line
down the middle of the road.

In tackling questions of this kind I naturally co-operated
closely with my colleagues: colleagues from the Commonwealth, colleagues like the heads of the Swedish and Japanese
Missions, and, above all, with my American and French
opposite numbers and commandants. I would often go out to
talk things over with them or with Brandt. The atmosphere
was always very friendly, though with no lack of frankness.
The United States Commandant, Major-General Al Watson,
and his wife, became great friends of ours. Al is about fifty-
three, tough, cheerful and reasonable, sure to go far. An
excellent horseman, he was modest about this as about all his
accomplishments. He disclaimed political experience and
originality of thought, but he was never petty, had a genuine
warmth of heart, and was always ready to take calculated
risks. I was delighted to see recently his promotion to the rank
of Lieutenant-General and his appointment to an important
command in the United States. The United States Minister
and his wife, Allen and Dottie Lightner, also became great
friends of ours. Allen was good to work with, a man of
imagination with great experience of Berlin.

I also admired the French team, who tended to plough
their own furrow, no doubt because they were under orders
to do so. (Did General de Gaulle really say : *'Mais Berlin est
foutu, non'?*) Even so they collaborated most effectively, often
putting their fingers unerringly on a crucial point overlooked

by the rest of us and dealing with it with quiet efficiency. For example, the disused railway water-tower : a useless object on one of those tricky bits of ground that was *Reichsbahn*—and therefore East German—property but also in the French sector. One morning the letters DDR (the German equivalent of GDR) appeared, painted conspicuously on it. Everyone called for instant decisive action. The French Commandant was reminded that one of his predecessors, General Ganeval, had once blown up a tower that offended him. This time it was decided, apparently, to play it cool. Mysteriously, after what one assumed to have been long negotiations behind the scenes, the communists approached the French with a suggestion for a settlement. Nothing happened. Then one day, the first D was seen to have been deleted : and the legend on the useless tower read DR, for *Deutsche Reichsbahn*. The French had allowed the communists to make themselves look silly.

Of course, the closest of all my colleagues was the British Commandant, Jumbo Delacombe. I saw him daily during the whole of my time in Berlin until his departure in May 1962. He looked rather like a first world war officer. He had had little previous political experience; and I sometimes had to ease matters along with our French and American allies. For instance, the question of movement between the three Western sectors : the position should have been that, except in a purely formal sense, these were treated as one. But I remember I had to work fairly hard on Jumbo to get him to agree to the Americans carrying out certain very necessary patrols, with us, in the British sector. Still, he nearly always followed my advice on political matters, and on the face of it our collaboration was efficient and friendly. I remember one occasion on which we were ready, booted and spurred, to set off to see Brandt on a secret matter of some importance. A conscientious member

of the staff came in at that very moment with a long FO
telegram in the well-known style. 'On the one hand...on the
other...In conclusion, better not.' 'Jumbo,' I said, 'this telegram has just missed us before we take the action on which
we have decided. Don't you agree?' He agreed that his
telegram-reading eye had gone blind. We set off and did our
business successfully, sending appropriate explanations to the
FO *ex post facto*.

Jumbo seemed to be liked by his troops and was, in fact, a
good General Officer Commanding; but obviously the post of
Commandant in Berlin calls for more than these routine
soldierly qualities.

I think we need a different type of man as British Commandant in Berlin. There are several able Major-Generals
who have had political experience in the many joint civilian-
service bodies in Whitehall and in commands abroad and who
would also be suitable by reason of their drive and enterprise.
I was told that one, a personal friend of mine who had all
these qualities, was turned down by Kit Steel because he was
too firm with Germans! HM Minister in Berlin should have
been able to guide him on that, if required. The American
system of selection, not only of commandants but of force and
troop commanders, is good. They send tough, seasoned, go-
ahead officers who are effective both militarily and politically.
Al Watson and his force commander, Brigadier-General Fritz
Hartel, as well as their numerous subordinate officers, admirably displayed these qualities.

As for our troops, and the regrettably small RAF contingent, they were first-class. They had an important and tricky
job to do, and they did it most effectively. They are much
liked, and most hospitably treated, by the Berliners. Their
position is altogether happier than that of the BAOR.

As head of what is called by tradition British Military

Government, I had under me a splendid staff, far more experienced than that of any of our allies though certainly less numerous than the complement of American officials in Berlin. Some of them had fetched up in Berlin to fill posts for which they were well qualified. Others were regular members of the Foreign Service. George Turner, our Information Officer, knew everyone in the Berlin press world. His only fault was a tendency to work himself to death, which I had to ask him to curb in the general interest. He would give me the technical and personal angle on a controversial article, though if it shed any light on communist policy I would turn to Paul Holmer, our expert on that subject. On legal posers Stephen Henry's shrewd, genial advice was at hand : he bubbled over with knowledge and energy. Geoff Edwards brought a keen analytical mind to bear on economic questions, and 'Tiny' Miles dominated the allied councils on all matters touching security. Guy Adams was a past master at dropping a word in the right ear so as to secure the co-operation of the Senate; and Ralph Banfield was able to manage both protocol and the oversight of Spandau gaol with the same mixture of calm and friendliness. As for Frank Waters, no British resident found him wanting in good cheer, and he kept a weather eye on trade as well. These men and their staffs, together with the half-dozen career diplomats, added up to a team of first-class calibre, unrivalled by any of our allies. I had under me the equivalent, in both numbers and quality, of the staff of one of our major embassies.

Together we had very various tasks to perform. There were the usual telegrams, sometimes as many as a score a day, from London, Washington, Bonn, some short and *en clair*, others running to hundreds of words in cypher on sheets of paper up to a yard long. Their subject matter ranged from the most minor details of administration to top secret discussions of current political and strategic policy. When I first arrived in Berlin I had found that we were kept none too well informed on major developments, and I insisted that if I was to do my job properly this should be remedied. We in turn had to report swiftly on urgent matters of policy or on actions taken. From time to time I departed from precedent and addressed these messages direct to the Foreign Office in London for instructions, taking care always to keep the British Embassy in Bonn informed. Although I gather Sir Christopher Steel was not best pleased by what he regarded as a slight on his position, I received no indication of disapproval from our joint superiors at the Foreign Office. We also received in the incoming bags copies of despatches and telegrams from all over the world, a system of communication which enables Our Man in Ouagadougou or San José to keep in touch. In our turn we had to prepare despatches on the economic progress of Berlin or the latest developments in the GDR, which I would approve before they went in the two weekly bags to Bonn and London. These were really background briefings, important but not urgent. In the old days a prodigious amount of time was lavished on these despatches, but in the Berlin of the Wall I discouraged them, preferring where possible crisp telegrams and personal letters.

I would also have to study the local intelligence and police reports and decide what action was called for. Sometimes this involved a visit to my friend Brandt; sometimes it required the Allied Kommandatura to be called together. But whatever it was I would discuss it with the Commandant and with my Counsellor and then take the appropriate action. A special skill was required in 'playing' the Kommandatura. When we had got our own British views clear on a particular problem, we would put it to one of the sub-committees of the Kommandatura: legal, economic, publicity, security and so on.

Where an agreed policy was possible—and it usually was—it would then go up to the Political Advisers (Counsellors); and the results would be submitted to the Ministers and Commandants. We should then either meet and discuss, or agree in writing or on the telephone. If everyone was agreed, a message would be sent back to all three Governments. But if any allied representative at any level had his doubts they would be referred to his Government for instruction.

The same procedure would be followed if the Berliners requested our approval of the extension of some piece of Federal legislation to Berlin. The request would go methodically through all the appropriate sub-committees before coming up to me and my oppos, or sometimes the Commandants, for final approval. This tripartite consultation was going on at some level every day of the week; and I came to feel a great respect for the Kommandatura machinery as far as the handling of routine matters was concerned. But when it came to crises and crash action it often proved hopelessly unwieldy.

I used to enjoy seeing journalists, British, American or German, and having discussions with them. Many members of the Foreign Service prefer to have nothing to do with journalists. They distrust them, think them congenitally inaccurate, slapdash, wilfully unreliable and incomplete in their information. In my experience the reverse is the case. I have learnt much from journalists and have come to admire their judgment and independence. The Foreign Office seems to be slowly waking up to some of these facts of life, but they still have a long way to go. In all this side of my work I had the great advantage of knowing German, the more so as my Commandant, Jumbo, did not. When I first arrived I had wondered how long the rust would take to polish off, but I found it came along better than I had expected. In fact, I dived in at the deep end by arranging to be interviewed in German on television, which was something of an innovation and gave me an opportunity of explaining to Berlin viewers what exactly my rôle in their city was.

This rôle, as I have explained, gave me a wonderful variety of parts to play, perhaps the strangest and most morbid of which was that of gaoler to the three remaining war criminals : Hess, von Schirach and Speer. Not that I want to exaggerate my share of responsibility. I was neither warder nor governor. But I was often invited to visit Spandau prison where these unfortunate men are still incarcerated and I did once have the macabre experience of taking lunch at the gaol. It is a fantastic situation : these three relics of history, pathetic creatures, all wickedness spent, inhabiting on their own what was once the gaol for all Berlin. Ironically the task of guarding them is now the only one (except for the Berlin Air Safety Centre) which remains in the hands of all four occupying powers. They take turns, month by month, in providing the chairman governor and the guards. The cells are good and so is the food; and the prisoners have a large garden in which to exercise. They looked fit enough to me, though Hess had a distinctly wild look in his eye. One of them said to me, almost gravely, that he had a request to make : he would like to go home, please. As far as the Western allies are concerned, they could all go home. They are costing a fair sum of money and taking up a great deal of room, and it is difficult to imagine them much of a danger to world peace. But the Russians are adamant.

Chapter 8

———

BERLIN CHARACTERS

All through these months the Wall had cramped and distorted the daily lives of the West Berliners and increased their bitterness. The flood of refugees from the East had been effectively stemmed. A few brave people continued to make their escape; crawling through narrow tunnels, swimming icy rivers and lakes, jumping from windows, crashing lorries and even trains through the obstructions. Many of them died in the attempt, victims of the almost subhuman cruelty of the East German police—the *Vopos*, the *Grepos*, and every other kind of *-po* (short for policeman). For instance, on the notorious Bernauerstrasse, in the French sector, the walls of the houses on one side form the actual sector border. In the early days men, women and children risked life and limb to jump from them on to the pavement or into waiting nets; some landed safely. The *Vopos* therefore walled up all the windows over a stretch of some hundreds of yards and evacuated all inhabitants from the houses. There are now many crosses in the Bernauerstrasse, in memory of those who died. Nor was it only the Wall which hemmed the East Germans in. There were also seventy odd miles of perimeter works, the extent

and murderous thoroughness of which had to be seen to be
believed. It was not just a matter of several lines of barbed
wire obstacles. A 'death-strip' had been cleared; which en-
tailed flattening everything within fifty yards or more—
houses, gardens, trees, graveyards. Often these strips were
mined; killer dogs were used to guard them; towers erected at
frequent intervals—exactly like those in the Nazis' concentration camps—helped to lessen the guards' chances of missing
their victims. Everywhere stood the scruffy-looking East German police and army, armed to the teeth and happy to shoot
at any of their compatriots who dared to appear in the wrong
place. They shot to kill. I made several trips round the perimeter, often with Dickie Richards. His method was to stop
the car a yard or two from any *Vopos* who were particularly
near the barbed wire and to shoot them—with his camera.
They often reacted by turning their backs in a shame-faced
manner; some adopted truculent attitudes. 'I suppose they'll
shoot me one day,' said Dickie meditatively. But they didn't.
To shoot non-Germans was not in their orders. By contrast the
West Berlin police invariably showed great restraint. But eventually, under extreme provocation, they picked off a *Vopo*
who, it transpired, was called Hermann Goering. The East
Germans gave him a hero's burial. There would have been
many more fatal incidents provoked by the *Vopos* if the West
Berlin police had not loyally obeyed the orders of the Western
allies and of their own Government, led by Willy Brandt.

Brandt is forty-nine, a large, friendly, sophisticated man
and a most able politician. He left Germany for Norway
during the war, married a Norwegian wife and fought on the
allied side : one of the few examples of genuine German resistance to Hitler. (I remember at one dinner party an aggressive
elderly Berliner of no importance telling me that he had been a
leader of the German resistance during the war and that it had

only failed because the allies would not support it. I turned my back on him.) It is quite extraordinary how seldom one meets a German who will even admit to remembering Hitler, let alone following him, but Brandt is not like this. He is one of the few Germans capable of acknowledging his country's past misdeeds, while working all the time for a happier future in Europe. Brandt is an admirable public speaker, though he always resists the temptation to play the demagogue. The Berlin crowds loved his gravelly voice. It would have been easy for him to have whipped up emotions in Berlin at the time of the Wall but he preferred to follow a firm line, balanced between exaggerated hope and despair. I have seldom seen him get excited either in public or in private. He is a stimulating companion with a good tough sense of humour, and lapses into a gloomy silence only when Dr Adenauer is in the room.

Politically, Brandt has grown in stature as he has moved from Marxism in the last two or three years. He is now second to Ollenhauer in the Social Democratic Party and in 1961 he campaigned for the Chancellorship with great success against Adenauer, a bitter and wily opponent. But above all Brandt stands for Berlin, and although the SPD (Social Democrats) have always defeated the CDU (Christian Democrats) in Berlin he has been prepared to collaborate loyally in a coalition with Adenauer's party for the benefit of the city. I am not sure that the CDU have always been quite as loyal. When Brandt went away, as he had to for short periods fairly often, to campaign for the Chancellorship or to represent his party at international gatherings, the CDU were not above suggesting that their leader, Mayor Amrehn, really ran the Berlin administration. This was not the case.

A striking and unfortunate example of CDU interference occurred recently when they prevented Brandt from accepting

Kruschev's invitation to go and see him during his visit to East
Berlin. Brandt would have gone, as he himself said, with no
illusions but with the hope that he could have impressed on
Kruschev some of the more monstrous effects of the Wall of
which Kruschev may well be ignorant. I am sure that nothing
but good could have come from a such a meeting. The CDU
attitude seems to have gone against them in the city elections
which came soon after, for the SPD gained a much larger
majority than before, and in fact an absolute one. (The communists received a minuscule vote, smaller than ever.) This has
given Brandt a freer hand, which is all to the good. The
SPD-CDU coalition had gone on for many years and was
becoming a bit stale. Brandt's idea of dropping the CDU in
favour of the FDP (Free German Party)—though they have
only a few seats—should bring some fresh air into the situation, and help him to shake off the CDU shackles back in
Bonn. The SPD-FDP combination might even be the pattern
for a future government of Germany.

    The Berlin Government's position was complicated by two
further factors. Though they were a lively and independent-
minded body, all major decisions and legislation were subject
to the approval of the Western allies. Secondly, Brandt was
always aware that his mean-spirited and arrogant opponent,
Dr Adenauer, was at work in Bonn on lines of policy that by
no means always served the best interests of Berlin.

    It is idle to speculate on what sort of a Chancellor Brandt
might make. But he is already an outstanding political figure,
whose reliability and good sense compare very favourably
with the qualities of his political rivals in Bonn, of whatever
party. If he continues at the rate he is going, that gap in
quality is likely to increase.

    I helped to organise Brandt's visit to Britain in March 1962.
He was very close to General Clay and some of his American

colleagues and had been two or three times to the USA. I decided the time had come for him to visit Britain too. The Labour Party had invited him and I was able to work out a good programme for him, combining certain political functions with official visits to the Foreign Secretary and the Lord Mayors of three or four cities in England and Scotland. Brandt is an excellent lecturer and he went down well with both press and television. The lunatic fringe on both left and right caused a few disturbances (they accused him of being both a communist and a Nazi). But he took all this in his stride. By the time I left Berlin I had come to know Brandt very well, both collaborating closely with him as mayor and cherishing a warm regard for him as a friend. There is an agreeable ceremony when a senior member of the Allied Kommandatura leaves Berlin. Brandt presents to him a replica of the Berlin bell of freedom, a copy of a famous American bell, with the inscription : 'That this world under God shall have a new birth of Freedom. Berlin 24.10.1950.' In view of my abrupt dismissal from the Foreign Service, it was not possible for me to enjoy this ceremony. I was very much touched that this arbitrary act did not prevent Willy Brandt from going to some trouble to send me, in London, my freedom bell, with my name duly inscribed, together with a fine piece of porcelain for my wife. The bell rests on my desk as I write.

I wish I admired Chancellor Adenauer as much as I admire Brandt. For some reason he had a distaste not just for Brandt, whom in the election campaign he abused in the grossest terms, but for Berlin as well which he manfully overcame to the extent of at least visiting the city some weeks after the Wall and being just about polite to Willy Brandt. Adenauer visited Berlin again during the British Fortnight, in which he showed no interest. This did not stop him making some very provocative remarks to the press about the question of Britain's entry into the Common Market. He gave, I remember, a stag dinner at which he was barely polite to Willy Brandt and very aggressive towards the allied Ministers and their governments' policies. I suggested lightheartedly that he should visit Kruschev in Moscow; but he replied that he had done so and that Kruschev could come to Bonn if he wanted to. As he said goodnight to me he remarked cryptically that British youth was dangerous and needed watching. I had no idea what he meant.

Of course Adenauer was no Berliner; indeed as a Rhinelander he had never liked the city and he found it a great effort to visit it. He came only three or four times during my stay there. I met him at the dinner parties he gave for leading Berliners and allies. On the last occasion, in May last year, he announced after dinner that he proposed to 'attack the diplomats'; and we middle-aged Ministers were lined up like schoolboys. He then indulged in half an hour's barbed badinage about our governments' policies which we answered as best we could. It was an amazing performance, especially as *Der Alte* did it all standing, as stiff as a ramrod, but the arrogance was excessive; and one could not help remembering —and regretting—how great a part that arrogance was playing and would continue to play in world politics.

Adenauer did a job of great importance in nurturing the delicate plant of German democracy after the war. But when, at over eighty, he had the chance of becoming President, he appeared to think he was indispensible as Chancellor and he descended to vulgar personal abuse of his opponent, Brandt, so that he could prolong his Chancellorship still further. Once having won with a majority narrower than before he indulged in undignified wrangles in order to escape the fate of retiring before he was ninety. Since then the scandal over *Der Spiegel*,

with its implication of Gestapo methods, has led to the resig-
nation of his friend the Defence Minister, Herr Strauss, and
the Chancellor's promise to retire 'next autumn'. We shall
see whether either of these gestures amounts to a row of beans.
All Adenauer's behaviour in the last couple of years has
worked directly against the strengthening of democracy which
he formerly fostered. The *Spiegel* affair is an outstanding
example, but there have been many others. It is chilling to read
that Speaker Gerstenmaier, normally a measured man, has
stated that if democracy is not flourishing it is not the Germans' fault, but the Russians. I seem to remember that Hitler
was not the Germans' fault either, but the fault of the Ver-
sailles Treaty.

Early in 1962, the Russians began playing a game in the
air corridors which could have proved very dangerous if the
West had not played it coolly back. They took to giving
notice to the Western allies of flights of Soviet military planes
which deliberately clashed with allied services, whether civilian or military. They tried everything from reserving in
advance great blocks of time and airspace to individual buzz-
ings of allied planes; they even dropped some 'chaff' or
'window'—tinfoil designed to upset radar direction-finding
apparatus.

The allied response to all this was the best co-ordinated bit
of work I remember during my time in Berlin, and this was
primarily because General Norstad, an outstanding example
of a truly supra-national figure, just as capable of counter-
manding an American initiative in Berlin as anyone else's,
took a directing hand. Inside Berlin the Western representatives in the BASC worked most efficiently. Sometimes we
would file counterplans to the Russians' entailing allied flights
at exactly the same time, place and height as theirs; occasionally if necessary we could alter a civilian flight by five or ten

minutes; but we always refused to accept any 'block pre-emption' of flying space. We also entered severe protests against the dropping of 'chaff', though it was on a small and ineffectual scale. There were some dangerous moments and some near misses; but the Russians never came near disrupting the morale of either the civilian or military Western pilots or their passengers and after several weeks they called it off.

In case the Russians should consider a repetition of such things, as they might at a later date, it is worth reminding them of something they already know : that our ability to break any attempted blockade is undoubted. We could now mount a vastly greater airlift than in 1948–49; and West Berlin holds stocks of essentials for keeping life, including industry, going for at least a year. Any form of communist interference in the air corridor could be overcome, though in some cases the price might be high. This capability is a useful deterrent to thoughtless action by the communists.

One point on which the East German authorities constantly lay great emphasis is that West Berlin is used by the Western Powers as a centre for espionage and for subversive action and propaganda. They brought this up with force during the 1959 negotiations. In 1962 again they issued a short book full of 'documentary' evidence including reports, photographs, addresses of agents and so on. Even in Ulbricht's latest TV appeal to the West Berliners, presumably intended to be con-ciliatory, he returned to the theme that these activities must cease before West Berlin could become a 'Free City', imply-ing of course that he would have to check up first to make sure they had ceased !

The allegations are highly misleading. Many of the docu-ments and so on in the latest publication look authentic enough, such as the photograph of the American tunnel under the Red Army's communications centre which was discovered some time ago. Equally, the names of some of the intelligence agencies which operate in Berlin such as the Central Intelligence Agency and some Federal German agencies which interrogate refugees, are correct.

But the impression which this book (published in Moscow), and GDR spokesmen, try to convey is quite incorrect. This is that half the population of West Berlin are constantly concerned with espionage and intelligence matters. (I only wish our intelligence on Ulbricht's intention to build the Wall had been better!) Also, they offer little firm evidence of such activities in the last two or three years, though there are allegations about activities connected with the Wall.

I happen to have had a good deal to do with intelligence in my time. I can vouch for the fact that the British intelligence-gathering activities in Berlin were perfectly above-board efforts to collect information about any hostile dispositions or intentions : active espionage as such did not come into the picture, much less any attempts to subvert the citizens of the GDR. On a basis of reciprocating with the Russians our own and our allies' military carried out two types of touring during which they, again like the Russians, naturally kept their eyes open. One consisted of trips by military motor-cars, with uniformed personnel, across the Wall. Naturally these were tailed on both sides, and if the home side considered that too much snooping was going on they indicated it firmly to the snoopers. The other variety was carried out by the British, and also American and French, Military Missions to the Soviet C-in-C of the Group of Soviet Forces in Germany. The allied missions, again consisting exclusively of uniformed personnel in military cars, were allowed under an agreement dating from soon after the war to drive around the Soviet Zone. However,

they were subject to all kinds of vexatious controls and pro-
hibitions by the Soviet authorities; and in recent years the
GDR authorities have taken a hand, without the slightest
right to do so. Thus an RAF corporal driver was shot and
very nearly killed in 1962 when driving an army colonel about
his lawful occasions. In return the Russians roam around the
three western sectors which now compose the whole of Federal
Germany. I regret to say that they are not as closely super-
vised as their allied opposite numbers; and when the allied
missions are mishandled or otherwise ill-treated we seldom
retaliate in kind, though on the occasion of the RAF corporal's
shooting I expressed the strong hope that we would.

One of the organisations which the East German authorities
constantly accuse of subversion is RIAS (Radio in the American Sector). This is a hard-hitting, but by no means subversive, radio station which gets under the communists' skin
owing to the force of its broadcasts to the GDR. Any demands
to curb it or do away with it should be firmly resisted. The
same applies to the official Berlin radio station, Sender Freies
Berlin.

As for good old-fashioned spying, as far as I know very little
of this is carried out by the allies in Berlin. The treasonable
activities of George Blake, who served in Berlin shortly before
he was uncovered, dealt a severe blow to our, and no doubt
our allies', intelligence-gathering; while in Berlin he was in
close touch with the communists.

In sum, the GDR's accusations on this score spring from
their own mentality. They and their world-wide communist
allies put espionage and subversion high on the list of international political weapons, as we know all too well. The
allegations are, in fact, a smokescreen. The answer is obvious.
We have any amount of information about East German
espionage : if they insist on checking up on activities in West

Berlin, it must be in return for a free hand for the Western
authorities to check up on East Berlin. But in the intelligence
world there is a sort of honour amongst rivals, partly cynical
but in many ways admirable. In the last resort nobody appre-
ciates Ulbricht poking his snout into these matters. As part
of any political negotiations over the Berlin problem as a
whole we need not take such allegations seriously.

Chapter 9

BERLIN VISITORS

A diplomat is on duty right round the clock. It is not just a matter of his keeping office hours. He has to be perpetually on the *qui vive*, attending official receptions and entertaining visitors. We in Berlin had more than our share of this, for the unique position of the city, shut off from the free world and yet a shop window for its goods and virtues, demanded that we should encourage men of every nation to see for themselves what the city was up against. Of course, a diplomat should be able to take this duty in his stride; he should be trained to it. But it doesn't leave too much time for relaxation. I tried to get in a good walk every day and I played an occasional game of tennis; and we much enjoyed the company of family and friends, the city's music and museums and our own books and pictures. But the greater part of our spare time as well as our working day was given over to representing Britain at some function or other directly or indirectly connected with the life of Berlin. I do not complain : personally, I relished the challenge and enjoyed doing my job as best I could. But it called for a great deal of stamina—and not from me alone. Elizabeth, too, though she did not have to come to the office and had an excellent domestic staff, was occupied full time attending every kind of official function as well as arranging our own private entertaining and looking after the running of the house.

Sometimes, though, returning from some rather dreary function, I was inclined to wonder cynically whether all this vigorous social life really paid off. Much of the entertaining exchanged in the diplomatic world has a slightly automatic tinge; and some of it is undoubtedly designed merely to keep boredom at bay. At the same time, as in the world of commerce, a good deal of it helps to establish the friendly relations which enable business to be done more smoothly. Young people considering the Foreign Service as a career ought to reckon that, in a sense, they will be on duty almost all the time—which is one reason why they will get quite generous tax-free allowances when they are abroad.

As I have said, a by-product of the critical situation in Berlin was the steady stream of visitors, from private tourists to VIPs, who poured into the city to see what was going on. They often seemed to make a point of turning up at the weekend, but whenever it was we set ourselves out to entertain them as best we could. Many of them came to stay, many more to drinks and meals; and I would lay on a variety of tours of inspection. The Wall, of course, was a 'must'; and other sights we liked to show them were the death traps round the perimeter, and the Eastern sector. As often happens we found it was one way of getting out to see these things for ourselves.

Sometimes we were able to offer our guests a taste of diplomacy and high politics as well. I remember one evening, shortly after the Wall had gone up, giving a dinner party for our old friends, Dolly and Bobby Burns. (He is a distinguished surgeon and she the daughter of Lord Duveen, benefactor of the Tate Gallery.) The other guests included the American Commandant, Al Watson, and his wife, as well as the Mayor of Berlin, Herr Amrehn, who was Brandt's deputy, and his wife. During the afternoon there had been rumours that the East German authorities, who for historical reasons still run the railways in West Berlin, both those inside the city and the long-distance services running into the GDR and connecting up with those in Federal Germany, were planning some surprise *coup*. Any move on their part would put us in a difficult position, for if either the West Berliners or the Western allies took any action against railway property it could, with some justification, be condemned as illegal by the East German authorities; moreover, they held the whip hand since they were in sole control of both the rolling stock and the permanent ways, and that included the military trains used by the allied troops to ply between Berlin and the Federal Republic. During dinner notes were brought in to both Al Watson and myself by members of our staffs; and Amrehn was called to the telephone more than once. Finally we held a council of war in a corner of the room. Amrehn had pretty reliable information that the Eastern authorities were going to hi-jack a large quantity of rolling stock from West Berlin before 2 a.m. that night. So we decided that the three allied Commandants and their Ministers must meet at midnight, with Amrehn and his advisers, in the offices of British Military Government, since they were the most central. Al Watson and I went off to the meeting. Our house guests went to bed, delighted with the raree show. Of course, the meeting went on and on as such meetings usually do, until we heard that no rolling stock had been removed nor, for various good reasons, could any be that night. There was some inclination to prolong the meeting; and I remember remarking that the communists were gaining points so long as we continued to wear ourselves out, and we should do better to recover our strength for the morrow.

This was only one of many official nocturnal activities. The communists liked stirring things up in the dark and we had to keep an eye on, and counter, all such enterprises. If some shooting or other attempt seemed to have serious implications we would go to the spot, whatever the time of night or day. Our allies were ready at all times to consult and confer. We had frequent tripartite alert practices at the most inconvenient hours, and often co-opted the West Berlin police. Military exercises, complete with their public relations and political activities, would go on for days and nights on end in and around the Grunewald. There was no let up.

We always liked to take visitors from England to see the Eastern sector of Berlin. Even before the Wall was put up, we British had followed the reasonable practice of showing our identity cards to the East Germans on duty at the crossing-points, while refusing to let them actually handle them : we found then that we were allowed through without any difficulty. Behind the Wall, the ordinary East Berliners seemed to move around quite normally, though they always appeared to be sunk in a sort of hopeless apathy. Although they were not well-dressed they were not, apparently, poverty-stricken, but there was a greyness everywhere, a listlessness as of people with nothing satisfying to live for. A great deal of rubble had been cleared away since our last visit to Berlin seven years before, though a great deal still remained : no one, evidently, was going to exert himself far in that direction. Where there had been signs of energetic clearance, they were invariably for purposes of prestige and propaganda. The large, beautifully kept Soviet war memorial park, for instance, with its heavily monumental statuary; and the large square where Ulbricht

and his friends delivered their long harangues at almost un-
endurably dull mass meetings. Far and away the most pathetic
effort at a show-place was the Stalinallee, now called the
Marx-Engelsstrasse. This was built by the Russians, when
mountains of rubble still littered the streets of East Berlin,
just to show the capitalists how grand were the shops and
flats and parks of the new privileged class, the faithful Party
members. In fact, it is like nothing so much as a fourth-rate
Oxford Street : the road is wide but the buildings are pathetic.
Very soon after they were put up they began falling down,
and by now they looked distinctly shoddy : a pretentious
monument to communist architecture. Some of the shops
were not too bad, but for the local inhabitants there was
always a catch of some kind—the shoes you wanted would
cost you a month's pay or the camera could be supplied only
in a year's time. The best buys were undoubtedly books and
gramophone records, but while these may have pleased the
tourists they can scarcely have sustained the lives of the East
Berliners. The food everywhere was appallingly dull and
limited, nothing like as plentiful as it should have been in
what was, after all, a highly agricultural state.

But the picture was not all black, or even grey. The
Pergamon museum still contained many works of art of high
quality and was run in a civilised way. The enchanting 18th
century opera house had been well restored, though the standard of performance had deteriorated with the flight of many
of the best singers to the West. The ordinary East Berliners,
too, were quite friendly. But I remember most vividly four
small children asking our car driver if he would put them in
the boot of the car and take them into West Berlin. There was
no suggestion in their manner that they had been put up to
make this touching plea. We made many trips to the Eastern
sector during our time in Berlin; and I made a special point

of taking visitors, official and private, with me whenever I could. It was one of the best ways of feeling the real atmosphere of the divided city.

Whenever possible we would then take the dirty taste out of our mouths by motoring on several miles northwards into the French sector, which, as one would expect, was impregnated with their own individual, highly civilised culture. Their headquarters, the Quartier Napoléon, is beautifully laid out, they have built a small modern cinema called L'Aiglon, and the Pavillon du Lac, where we would usually lunch, is a good modern building with fine views over the Tegelsee. Quite near there is the airfield from which they run the only jet service to Berlin, using their own Caravelles.

Among the visitors who came to Berlin in my time I remember Hugh Gaitskell with special pleasure. When he arrived as the guest of the Berlin Government I was acting as Commandant during Jumbo's absence. Brandt, who seemed to get on specially well with him, gave a dinner at which more forward ideas than usual were aired about the Berlin negotiations, in particular the question of recognising the GDR. To my surprise—and gratification—General Clay asked if he might come and meet Gaitskell in my office. It was the only time during his stay in Berlin that the General came to our Headquarters. Gaitskell welcomed the proposition and the press displayed such keen interest that I asked both my guests whether they would mind being televised. They did not seem to mind at all; and the whole affair went off well, everyone shaking hands, smiling and chatting away in the most convincing fashion. The hour's discussion was most constructive, and none of the difficulties which I had anticipated materialised. The divergence of view between the two of them did not seem to obtrude in the slightest.

The following week the British Foreign Secretary, Lord

Home, came on from Bonn with Sir Christopher Steel and Sir Evelyn Shuckburgh, the top Foreign Office expert on Berlin, arriving before dinner one day and leaving after lunch the next. Never mind. The Ambassador gave a working dinner for him, at which various notables were present. The following morning Willy Brandt conducted a tour of the Wall and other horrors. He insisted on taking Lord Home and his party to the very top of the burnt-out Reichstag building in the British sector. The last two stages of the ascent involved climbing almost perpendicularly up builders' ladders : very strenuous and somewhat perilous. But it was worth it, for the views from the top embrace a large part of the Eastern sector.

At lunch I remember Lord Home making a typical speech —entirely individual, utterly sincere, altogether engaging. Afterwards I insisted on his touring the perimeter of the British sector, since the horrors of the death traps set up there were less well known than those of the Wall.

After this visit General Clay returned to the city from a visit to Washington. Others besides myself could not help wondering whether he had deliberately avoided Lord Home's visit. In my curiosity I asked to be allowed to call on him to exchange views. I was snubbed. From then onwards General Clay mingled very little with his allies, even socially, and I have reason to believe that he also became increasingly difficult towards his own compatriots. Reconstructing this curious episode, I can only conclude that Clay had wanted to press on with the forward policy he had so clearly pushed in the October tank manoeuvres. This had not only been criticised by some of the allies in Berlin, as we had reported to our governments, but he had also forfeited the support of his own government. I suspect that he must have been told to pipe down while he was in Washington, possibly being told, to soften the blow, that this was suggested largely at the instigation of his colleagues in Berlin. At any rate, from then on, when we met socially he was polite but certainly not warm towards Elizabeth and myself. And towards the French Commandant, General Lacomme, and Jumbo, when they went to pay their farewell visits, he was only just polite. None the less, he continued to collaborate closely with Brandt and the Berlin Government and switched his efforts towards encouraging American economic support for Berlin. No doubt he had been given a new brief in Washington. I did not let this curious behaviour lessen my respect for him and his work for Berlin; and both Elizabeth and I continued to enjoy the Clays' company.

In May 1962 General Clay was removed. I was told that he received orders to leave Berlin from the President at almost the same moment as his withdrawal was made public in Washington. He was furious. At any rate, he departed without any official allied farewells. He saved some face with the announcement that he would continue to act as a special adviser to the President on Berlin. I believe he has since been back a couple of times. I couldn't help thinking that this whole episode revealed a rather churlish treatment of a distinguished man who had done a very good job under instructions. Later I came to reflect that Berlin was really rather hard on the reputations of allied government servants and their careers. The French Commandant and his Minister had both been whisked away in the night; and when the blow fell in my own case I dubbed myself, not without a sort of wry pride, 'the poor man's Clay'.

Among heads of state who came our way was President Abboud of the Sudan and our old friend from Cyprus days Archbishop Makarios. We had come to know him pretty well, first from the maddening negotiations which led to independence, when such stirring subjects as the price of a packet of

cigarettes at the NAAFI could take up to three days to settle,
and later when, as Head of State, he co-operated loyally and
sensibly with us in the British Sovereign Base Areas. He made
a very good impression in Berlin. In his official speech he said
that Cyprus was an 'uncommitted' country but he strongly
condemned the Wall and left no one in any doubt where his
true feelings lay. On the day of his arrival the *Vopos* gave one
of their choicest performances when they put fifteen bullets
through a boy of fourteen who was swimming across the
border to freedom. He got across somehow, and miraculously
survived. The Archbishop went out of his way to interrupt his
very full programme and visit him in hospital. People in
England who used to think of Makarios as a bloodthirsty,
double-crossing gunman in priests's clothes would be disarmed
by the kindliness and consideration for others which mark
this strange many-sided man.

Life became quite hectic when, on top of the routine work
and the special measures we had to take at times of crisis, we
found ourselves acting as a sort of semi-permanent reception
committee with a special line in guided tours round the
Berlin hot-spots (I do not mean the night clubs). Ministers
and MPs would call on us in large numbers. As well
as Lord Home I remember Peter Thomas coming out,
and staying with us. The next time I was to see him
was as spokesman explaining the Foreign Office's reasons
for my retirement. We particularly enjoyed having Sir Keith
Joseph to stay. He was nice enough, I remember, to say what a
good advertisement for Britain was provided by our home
and our representational activities. Among back-benchers,
the most helpful was certainly Victor Goodhew. While
he was with us taking a general look at the Berlin
scene he undertook a most useful mission. A young English-
man had got himself caught by the *Vopos* trying, not very

skilfully, to smuggle a girl out of the Eastern sector into West Berlin. We were powerless to help. We approached the Soviet Commandant, who promptly referred us to the 'sovereign' GDR authorities. As a matter of high policy we were not allowed to deal with them. I discussed the case with Goodhew, who volunteered to take up the cudgels. Accompanied by the intrepid Frau Kerr, a high-grade interpreter employed by the Berlin Senate, he went into the Kafka-land of East German officialdom. He was there a long time. First, he was told the prisoner did not exist, then that if he did exist he was not known to that particular Ministry, etc, etc. After forty-eight hours of this sort of maddening performance the hapless man was produced and allowed to have a short talk with Goodhew, who had been a model of patience. He seemed in good shape, and he was released very shortly afterwards, although his sentence had been a long one. One up to Goodhew, I thought.

On the other side of the House, as well as Gaitskell I had the pleasure of entertaining his deputy, George Brown. Frank Cousins came on another occasion with a TUC delegation. I remember this visit well. It was a sunny Sunday morning before lunch, the lake looked lovely and the drinks were good. I had the idea of mixing the top trade unionists up with some visiting airmen : the Chief of the Air Staff, Air Chief Marshal Sir Thomas Pike, and the Air C. in C. RAF in Germany, Air Marshal Sir John Grandy, among them. Frank Cousins is not exactly a military type, but my little experiment came off and there was no anti-nuclear explosion.

I do not want to give the impression that we did nothing in Berlin but talk politics and pour drink down visitors. There was in fact a flourishing cultural life in Berlin, and Elizabeth and I enjoyed it to the full. We used to like especially our visits to the Opera House, and we welcomed singers and

others to our home. One visitor from England whom I had
not seen since he had come out to Chile twelve years before
was Sir Malcolm Sargent, who was conducting the Berlin
Philharmonic Orchestra, and spent some of his time off
entertaining us with his sophisticated and witty conversation.
The British Council chief, Sir Paul Sinker, also came out to
open a new centre. We gave a dinner for him and some of the
intellectual leaders of Berlin, people connected with West
Berlin's two universities, with the Dahlem museum, the Opera,
and the various orchestras. Listening to all this excellent music,
and going to see the magnificent pictures and statuary in the
Dahlem museum, were great pleasures for us.

I cannot agree with all the British Council's policy in
Berlin. It is a complete illusion to think that they have any
essential part to play there. The Berliners are as cultured as
the next people, and they need no instruction from us; and
individual Berliners are perfectly capable of satisfying their
cultural curiosity about Britain from their own resources and
the support given by the Berlin authorities. But, above all,
Berlin is culture-conscious in a big way, with first-class
music and books, good theatres and cinemas, and virtually
unlimited funds for all such pursuits. The British Council's
centre and library are good; and they could well continue to
provide facilities for the teaching of English, though in fact
these can be easily found elsewhere in the city. But they
should certainly cut out all their penny-whistle concerts and
magic-lantern shows about Kent. If they have money to spare,
they should put it into two or three first-class performances
a year—by the Festival Ballet, say, or the Old Vic.

Chapter 10

FAREWELL TO BERLIN

The spring was nearly over, and although I did not know it my time in Berlin was drawing to its close. But first I had to say farewell to the Delacombes. They had been in Berlin three years, and before their departure on May 3 there was a continuous round of parties for five or six weeks. They had made themselves well liked. We gave a dinner for them and their family. Another dinner at which I presided was given by the entire senior staff of British Military Government, and I remember paying tribute in my speech for all that they had done in the city. In addition, of course, they had their Golden Book ceremony as well as a combined allied parade and a large dinner given by the Watsons. What with Jumbo off on the 3rd and his successor arriving the next day, the beginning of the British Fortnight, devoted to the promotion of British trade, and the visit of Sir Keith Joseph (then Minister of State at the Board of Trade), on top of the ordinary business of life, these were busy times. Also, the Steels came up for the week-end. I was mildly surprised not to be invited to any of the Steel-Delacombe get-togethers; but as the Delacombes went straight off on the 3rd to spend a couple of nights in

Bonn with the Steels, it is clear they had plenty to talk about by themselves. It was only later that I realised that my position must have been on their agenda. That I was lulled into a complete unawareness of the fate that lay in store for me was at least partly due to the Ambassador's action in going out of his way to congratulate me on the success of my collaboration with Jumbo. He remarked, I recall, that the new Commandant would depend heavily upon me.

We saw the Delacombes off at the *Autobahn* checkpoint. They were affable as ever; Jumbo kissed Elizabeth on the cheek, and I did as much to Joyce. As they drove off a colleague remarked that it must be sad for us to lose our friends in this way. We thought so too, we said. And we meant it.

A little later that month I delivered a fairly comprehensive lecture on the Berlin problem to both the Imperial Defence College and the Canadian Defence College, and with my 'brains trust' of senior British colleagues, answered many questions. I was already beginning to develop in my mind, and to discuss privately with one or two senior members of my staff, some rather unorthodox ideas about the solution of the Berlin problem. The discussions which these talks provoked encouraged me to think further, and later on to formulate suggestions for breaking the impasse over Berlin, which I outline in Chapter 12.

The day of our leave approached. It was too slow in coming particularly as, for the previous few weeks, Elizabeth had not been well. She was not by any means the only one to be worn down by the combination of intense official life and the claustrophobic atmosphere of the beleaguered city. We could not get her better there and I wanted to take her to see a specialist in London. And so we said goodbye, fully expecting to be back again in Berlin in mid-July. Our last day, June

I, was very active, for it was the Queen's Birthday. The British Army are good at ceremonial parades and all went very well. The horses behaved. Everyone was smartly turned out. I was proud to be entertaining our principal guests, while the new Commandant did his stuff on the parade ground. After the parade I had some talk with Willy Brandt, and then went on to a 'working' lunch with Allen Lightner, Brandt and the French Minister, Jean le Roy. At four o'clock Brandt had a long personal talk with me in his office. He gave me messages for the Foreign Secretary and hoped, he said, that I would stay a long time in Berlin.

And so to the packing and the preparations. After dinner I was told by the duty officer that a telegram had arrived for me from Sir Francis Rundall. It said an important letter was in the bag, due in three days' times, and it asked me to arrange to see it before leaving Berlin. I sought Sir Christopher Steel's advice in Bonn; and his reply, delivered through his private secretary, was that we would find a copy on our arrival in England, and, as for him, he had no idea of what was in it. Which, as we later came to realise, was rather rum.

Next morning we were seen off by several of our colleagues. Our journey was given over to speculation about the contents of the letter; we felt quite optimistic, half expecting some new, exciting post. By the time we reached München-Gladbach, where we were week-ending with friends, Elizabeth was already beginning to feel better. On the Monday morning she flew on ahead to spare herself the strain of the motor and air ferry journey. When she got to our London hotel she was handed a letter by the porter. She opened it (naturally I had asked her to open it, if it arrived before I did). She read that Jumbo Delacombe had recently told the Permanent Under-Secretary at the Foreign Office, Sir Harold Caccia, that I had not been fully co-operative, and that Sir Christopher Steel had

complained about me a few months before. I was to leave
Berlin and to retire from the Service under the 1943 Act.
Elizabeth was thunderstruck. No one could have known that
the letter would be opened by anyone but me, but even so
it seems to me that the Foreign Office presented the news in
a devious and clumsy way. Elizabeth stood up to the blow
well, and told me about it on the telephone. I thought it best
to keep the news to myself for the time being, though the
strain was considerable. That afternoon I drove and flew to
London, my mind a whirl of unpleasant thoughts and ideas.
What could be the explanation? Why had I had no inkling?
What should I do now? The questions raced through my
mind.

Chapter 11

THE McDERMOTT CASE

The months since the blow fell on us have not been easy. We are not people who enjoy publicity. But we knew and our friends knew that justice had not been done, let alone seen to be done; and so we refused to take it lying down not simply for our own sakes, but so that some light might be cast on the administrative workings of the Foreign Office, for the benefit of the Service. We decided to let the truth be known, and we received great encouragement from our friends inside and outside the Service, from the press, and from leading Opposition spokesmen in both Houses of Parliament.

But first, in June and July, we aimed at getting Elizabeth well; and we succeeded remarkably soon. Then, we had to find somewhere to live in London, as we had sold our Kensington house the year before, expecting to be abroad for some time. Here again we succeeded and on July 4 we moved into the flat which we had taken to at once and have come to love more and more. I write now on a glass-covered veranda with a view beneath of Crewe House with its beautiful garden, and beyond of the splendid new Park Lane Hilton Hotel.

At the same time I had to go through the process of defending myself against the Foreign Office's accusations. The letter of June 1 went into the technicalities of the procedure for retirement under the 1943 Act. This Act is a short one and is not very specific about the retirement procedure. However, the White Paper which accompanied it indicated that it gave the Foreign Secretary discretion to retire, on a pension, members of the Service who had shown signs of slowing up and, for one reason or another, no longer being able to cope with their duties. It has, in fact, been applied infrequently over the years; and up till my case its application has caused little if any surprise to Foreign Service colleagues of the victim. After all, some people in every walk of life tend to go slower than others in their forties or later. But what the Act was not intended to provide was a handy means of removing someone whose energies remain unimpaired but whose methods might seem too unorthodox or go-ahead for some of his senior colleagues.

The procedure under the Act was as follows: first, a memorandum had to be prepared in the Office and presented to the Senior Promotions Board. If this board decided to proceed further, it had to make a report to the Retirement Board, which consisted of three distinguished men outside the Service. I had the right to comment either in writing or in person, or both, to a committee of the first Board. I decided to comment only in writing. I have been criticised for this, as though I lacked confidence in my own case. But I had several good reasons. The day after the letter arrived I had rung up Sir Francis Rundall, the Chief Clerk. Tony Rundall had been a friend of mine for many years. But on this occasion I found he had little to say to me. When I pointed out that I had received no warning of any kind, he said abruptly that I had —in 1947—and that should have been sufficient. He added that of the people so far arraigned under the 1943 Act only one had defended himself successfully; 'and we got him out later,' he added significantly.

This was one reason for my decision—the evident inevitability of my 'retirement'. Another was personal : I wished to spare embarrassment to those of my personal friends who would be sitting on the Committee and thus confronting me in the dock. A personal friend who is a very senior member of the Service supported me in this. Even if you win, he said, it will be unsavoury consulates-general for you from now on. Finally, my letters to the Foreign Secretary and the Permanent Under-Secretary asking for interviews with them must have reached them two or three weeks before and it was reasonable to expect replies. These, however, never came. I was assured, too, that full weight would be given to my written comments. And this proved true up to a point, for the final indictment, with my comments, bore scarcely any resemblance to the first one and was a very feeble affair by comparison. For instance, one of the charges initially preferred against me, believe it or not, related to the publication of the first *Observer* story. This, of course, had to be dropped. And so did much more serious, and equally ill-founded charges : that I was late clocking in at the office, took too much leave and was beastly to my staff. All were sunk without trace. However, the Retirement Board to whom the watered-down charge sheet was sent, which included Lord Strang and Sir Harold Nicolson, had no comment to make; and the Foreign Secretary, on the strength of it, approved my retirement on September 15, with a pension of around £1,400 a year and a lump sum of £4,000 odd— what one might call a pewter handshake. Shortly afterwards the appointment of my successor was leaked to the press : a very sound man, a personal friend of Steel's, who was promoted from being a counsellor on his staff for the purpose.

Before all this had gone through, we felt a great need of sun and relaxation; so we flew off with our two young sons to Corfu. While there I decided to try my hand at a couple of articles. I found my ideas were beginning to crystallise and I later knocked the two articles into one. As we lay on the beach in the great heat the bureaucratic machine in London was grinding on. I had a letter from the Foreign Office referring to my 'forthcoming retirement' and asking me to 'make every effort to complete the allocation procedure [for my pension] without delay'. This seemed a curious form of prejudgment showing, I thought, scant respect for either the Retirement Board or the Foreign Secretary, to whom the question of my retirement had yet to be submitted. A few days later I received the memorandum intended for them, and I sent back my comments on it. We returned to London at the end of August and shortly afterwards I was told that everything was now tied up, and the date of my retirement had been fixed as September 15.

A few days later I showed the article I had written in Corfu to a friend on *The Observer*. He liked it, and *The Observer* accepted it. In their issue of September 23 it was spread over both leader pages, and I was rather pleased with the effect of my first piece of journalism. It attracted a good deal of attention on both sides of the iron curtain. It was reprinted whole in a Canadian newspaper, and one American paper gave a summary of it headed 'A Burst of Sanity'. It led directly to my being invited to write other articles and deliver a number of lectures. No less than seven publishers, two of them American, asked me to write a book.

All this made it clear to me that my views were a matter of public interest. But it had also become clear that many of my friends, as well as others in various spheres including journalists, were much puzzled at my sudden withdrawal from

the diplomatic scene. Out of loyalty to the Service in which
I had spent more than twenty-six years, Elizabeth and I said
as little as possible about what was going on so long as the
'case' remained *sub judice*. We fobbed off friends and journalists alike with half-truths. However, *The Observer* had pieced
a good deal of the story together for themselves, and on
another page of the issue which carried my article on Berlin
they published the following in their 'Daylight' column, written
by 'Pendennis'. The story was headed : EXIT A DIPLOMAT.

'Six years ago,' it began, 'Geoffrey McDermott, whose inside story on Berlin appears on page 10, was the youngest
Minister in the Foreign Service. Until June he was Our Man
in Berlin. Last week, at 49 years of age, he was suddenly,
silently, prematurely "retired".

'McDermott, to put it at its lowest, is a man of talent. Two
Firsts at Cambridge. Fluent French and German. A succession
of tough assignments culminating first in two years as Political
Representative with the Middle East Forces based on Cyprus
and, finally, in his term as British Deputy Commandant in
Berlin with the specially enhanced status of Minister.

'He is in fact something of a trouble-shooter, unconven-
tional, not a man to suffer fools gladly but a man of spirit who
has always got on specially well with military men. Most
people would be glad to go tiger shooting with him. But not
Major-General Sir Rohan (Jumbo) Delacombe, lately the
British Commandant in Berlin. And not Sir Christopher (Kit)
Steel, the British Ambassador in Bonn.

'Being the sort of frank, friendly (and wealthy) man who
falls on his feet, McDermott soon found a splendid house, a
marble *palazzo* (formerly the Netherlands Embassy) with a
lake in the garden. There he entertained as no Deputy

Commandant had ever entertained before. In a very short while his outgoing temperament had got him on good terms with the American and French Commandants, with General Clay and Willy Brandt, the Governing Mayor of West Berlin.

'Jumbo Delacombe would have been only human if he had felt an occasional twinge of envy at his colleague's success. But he never showed it and he never once complained at McDermott's handling of affairs.

'The refugees were pouring in from the East. In August the Wall went up. In October the Russian tanks were rumbling up to the Brandenburg Gate. Quick political judgments were needed. McDermott made them, taking care to send Steel, in Bonn, copies of his despatches to the Foreign Office.

'Kit Steel would have been only human if he had occasionally resented the way in which events (and McDermott) were passing him by. But he never showed it. Older than his 59 years and a stickler for the pomps and vanities of the diplomatic round, Steel would go to Berlin every six weeks or so and with what passed for *sang-froid* would spend part of his time on the golf course.

'Late last May, Jumbo Delacombe went home into retirement. On the way he took the opportunity of privily lodging a complaint about McDermott's behaviour with Sir Harold Caccia, the Permanent Head of the Foreign Office. A few days later Steel, on one of his visits to Berlin, went out of his way to commend McDermott for the way he had collaborated with the Major-General. Little did he know. Or did he?

'Early in June, McDermott went on leave. An urgent letter followed him telling of the complaint of lack of co-operation lodged against him without his knowledge. He also learned that it had been initialled, without calling for explanation, by Caccia.

'Although regulations lay down that complaints should

always initially be made face to face, in every other respect the set disciplinary procedure under the 1943 Act was followed meticulously with the secrecy of a Papal conclave. At each level reports—official indictments—were sent to McDermott, who elected throughout to comment in writing.

'The upshot was that he was fired, though the euphemism of "retirement" was preserved to the last. The official Foreign Office version of the affair is that he retired because of his wife's indifferent health and the "general conditions prevailing in the service at the present time for those of his grade". They have no knowledge of any dispute over Berlin Policy between McDermott and either Steel or the Major-General.

'However that may be, McDermott has taken his dismissal philosophically. A man of means, connected by marriage with Robertson's marmalade, he can afford to. But his fate, as it becomes known, seems likely to act as a warning to diplomats who are tempted to show too much independence and initiative.'

This account was extraordinarily near the mark. The same day on which the piece appeared a Foreign Office spokesman denied that I had been retired as a result of a disagreement over policy. He gave two reasons for my 'retirement': my wife's indifferent health, and the general situation in my grade which meant that there was only a limited number of posts to which I could be promoted. The provisions of the 1943 Act, he added, had been applied in the normal way for persons wishing to retire. I could not let this travesty of the true facts pass without correction. So I gave an interview to the diplomatic correspondent of *The Guardian* in which I made it clear that I had been forced to resign. I explained that I had been given no inkling from any quarter, until on June 4

I received Sir Francis Rundall's letter of June 1, of any dissatisfaction with my work in Berlin, though I acknowledged that I had had a reprimand in 1947 when I was preoccupied with divorce proceedings at the expense of my work. Elizabeth, I said, was in excellent health. (I had earlier agreed to the Foreign Office's suggestions that her illness might be given as a reason for our sudden withdrawal from Berlin; but certainly not for any other purpose.)

There was no comeback from the Foreign Office. But I will confess that I enjoyed reading in the press that: 'While in Berlin the 49-year-old diplomat was renowned for his dynamic and outgoing temperament,' and that I now made the impression of being 'vigorous ... remarkably frank for a diplomat—or rather, an ex-diplomat'; and that 'McDermott, I'm told, is an extremely able diplomat, who was a great success in Berlin. ... It is difficult to think of a more effective way of discouraging independence—and honesty—among our diplomats.'

I now learnt from some of my friends that my case was to be raised in Parliament. I was somewhat surprised, but they proved to be right. There was a month's lull, as Parliament was in recess. But on the day of reassembly, October 25, Mr Peter Thomas, Joint Parliamentary Under-Secretary at the Foreign Office, gave this written reply to a question by Mr Stephen Swingler: 'Mr Geoffrey McDermott was retired from the Foreign Service last month under the Foreign Service Act, 1943, which allows the Foreign Secretary to terminate on pension the careers of officers who, though they may have been satisfactory in the early years of their service, lose the qualities of initiative and energy which are necessary if they are to hold positions of greater responsibility.'

This new and still more astonishing version of the facts provoked a most indignant reaction. One person described it as 'character assassination'. Another questioned whether the spokesman had not meant to say of this curious class of officers, who are so satisfactory in their early days, that they have come to display '*too much* initiative and energy'. Yet another compared my qualities favourably with those being displayed all the time by several of the more elderly members of the Foreign Service. I myself pointed out how odd it was that the Foreign Office kept on publishing different, incompatible and inaccurate reasons for my 'retirement'. They had, after all, given me yet another set of reasons in their letter of June 1, and if these were the real reasons it seemed almost incredible that neither the Foreign Secretary, the Permanent Under-Secretary, Steel nor Delacombe had personally said or written a word to me either before or since their complaints were made.

Mr Gaitskell, amongst his innumerable preoccupations, now took up my case with force. He asked me to call on him in the House and, together with Mr Harold Wilson, devoted about an hour to a discussion of it. This confirmed their grave doubts about its justice, and on October 31 Mr Harold Wilson, speaking in the Debate on the Address as Opposition foreign affairs spokesman, referred to it as follows : 'While on the subject of resignations [he had just mentioned that of Sir Hugh Foot], we have also the strange case of Mr McDermott, late of Berlin, whom many Hon. Members know and respect. The Government owe the House a full explanation, because official statements are confusing and contradictory and until we have a full statement we cannot begin to say whether justice has been done; but we can certainly say today that it manifestly has not been seen to have been done.'

Later a debate took place on the adjournment on November 9. I went along to watch myself on the operating table; but what I saw was a carve-up of Mr Peter Thomas, the Foreign

Office spokesman, by Mr Harold Wilson. It was Mr Anthony Greenwood who raised the matter : he opened with a very sympathetic and comprehensive account of the case, including a survey of my career. After describing the ideas on the Berlin problem which I had put forward in my *Observer* article he ended by saying : 'Those views will command wide support in this House and throughout the country. Their constructive quality makes Mr McDermott's loss to the Foreign Service even more severe. I hope that the Under-Secretary today will be able to give a more satisfactory explanation than has yet been forthcoming of what I believe to be a serious injury to the Foreign Service as a whole and a grave injustice to an individual.'

Mr Thomas then rose to make his defence. (By this time it was no longer I who was in the dock.) He started by saying some nice things about me personally and about my abilities, but laid great emphasis on what he called 'a recurrent tendency' on my part to do less work than I might. He dismissed the period between 1947 and 1961, during which I became the youngest Minister in the Foreign Service, with the words : 'After this, his work improved. He went on to do the satisfactory work in the Foreign Office of which I have spoken earlier. Ten years later, after an inspection of Mr McDermott's post in Cyprus shortly after his departure for Berlin, it was again evident that he had not done his full share of the work in Cyprus where he had been head of the Political Office with the Middle East Forces.' Mr Thomas, who has the reputation of being a bright fellow, had clearly been badly briefed, for there were two inaccuracies here. This period was not ten years but more than thirteen. And the inspection in Cyprus took place while I was still there. He also stated erroneously that all five Foreign Office political Ministers had agreed to recommend my retirement to the Foreign Secretary.

He sidestepped the question whether I had ever been faced with complaints before the letter of June 1 was sent.

Mr Harold Wilson's rapid-fire reply, delivered in the three minutes left for debate, was masterly, and I venture to quote it in full:

'I sympathise with the Joint Under-Secretary of State. He was obviously embarrassed at having to put such a thin case before the House. It was one of the thinnest I have ever heard, and I want to put these questions. After all the claptrap that we had from the Hon. Gentleman about complaints in the 1940's and so on, why, if this was true, was Mr McDermott promoted twice since, including the unusual promotion to the rank of Minister at the age of forty-three? The Hon. Gentleman has not explained this.

'Secondly, if all that was true, why was Mr McDermott sent to such a notorious hot-spot as Berlin? If he was being considered for retirement because of all this long history which the Hon. Gentleman has scratched up out of the archives, why send him to Berlin? The Joint Under-Secretary must know that Berlin is one of the most vital places in the world to have one of our best people.

'Does the Hon. Gentleman agree that none of the complaints that were made about Mr McDermott when he was in Berlin were ever made to Mr McDermott? This is a serious point. If these complaints came either from the military or from our Ambassador in Bonn, why was he not told? Elementary justice demands it.

'There is, however, something much more sinister about this and we will get an explanation, either today or at some other time, from the Hon. Gentleman. Why were not the charges properly stated to Mr McDermott? It is all very well

to say that he had the right of appearing, but there was a
hopeless muddle about this procedure. I have been into this as
thoroughly as my Hon. friend the Member for Rossendale
(Mr Greenwood). The decision was taken. Mr McDermott
received a letter on June 7 telling him that the decision had
in principle been taken and that he could make retrospective
observation about it afterwards.

'That is not justice. The House of Commons is concerned
with justice. I am not concerned with whether Mr McDermott was an efficient officer. I assume that he was, or he
would not have been sent to Berlin or have been promoted
just before. What chance had he of giving a proper defence?
The Joint Under-Secretary knows that he has misrepresented
the facts, because when Mr McDermott mentioned the case
of his wife's health, he mentioned it as the reason for leaving
Berlin and not for leaving the Foreign Service.

'In a week in which there has been an orgy of White Papers,
in view of the highly unsatisfactory nature of the Hon.
Gentleman's reply today, I must ask him to ask his noble
Friend to present a White Paper giving all the exchanges and
complaints, the dates when they were made by the General
and by the Ambassador and the dates when the complaints
were initiated, formally and informally, to Mr McDermott.

'I hope that we will get a clear answer. There is no time
for it to be given today. The Joint Under-Secretary must
inform his noble Friend that this House is not satisfied with
the explanation which has been given and cannot agree either
that justice has been done or has been seen to be done. We
want a full White Paper, because the Opposition will certainly return to the subject.'

This debate received very full press coverage. It was just

about now that the newspapers began to refer to the McDermott 'saga'. The general conclusion seemed to be that there was something mysterious which the Foreign Office had not revealed and which, as Mr Wilson had said, the Opposition were determined to expose. In conversation I often heard it said that it was the violence of the Foreign Office's action which was so inexplicable. Why had they not simply offered me some outrageously unpleasant or unimportant post, which is a method they commonly employ to rid themselves of people whom they regard as tiresome?

When questioned by the press I would make two main points. One was that I was still in Cyprus when the inspector referred to by Mr Thomas called. He was a junior man on the sort of routine administrative inspection which is made periodically of all Foreign Service posts. We certainly discussed administrative matters, but I received not so much as a hint that he had reported that I was not working long hours in the office. I had, as I have said earlier, told the Foreign Office some time before that I was underemployed; almost all the 'top brass' in the Sovereign Base Areas were in the same situation. I remember hearing one person who was in a good position to know say that if anyone in Cyprus was working more than a few hours a day in his office he could only be wanting to create unnecessary work for other people. But, for some reason, this junior inspector's views were given more weight than those of Mr Julian Amery and General Sir Dudley Ward. Why, in any case, I would add, did the Foreign Office switch me to such a critical place as Berlin if they were so dissatisfied? They had plenty of time to alter my appointment after the inspection and the publication of the story in *The Observer*. The other point I kept reiterating was that I had never been faced with the charges against me, not even in the letter of June 1. Foreign Service regulation

Number 12, headed 'Disciplinary Questions', seemed relevant to my case : clause 4 (a) reads : 'Complaints of disciplinary offences by a member of the Service shall be made by the official superior in a letter addressed to the Under-Secretary of State for Administration setting out the full facts of the case. A copy of this letter shall be communicated to the person complained of either by the official superior or, if he has not done so, by the Under-Secretary of State for Administration, and at the same time the person complained of shall be reminded of the procedure described in this regulation.'

When this point was first made publicly it produced an immediate statement from a Foreign Office spokesman, who said, on November 12, that no disciplinary complaints were being made. These would have involved such matters as 'dishonesty, secrets and morals, and would entail dismissal'. I had not been dismissed but merely retired—they had long ago given up the pretence that I had 'resigned'—with a pension and a lump sum.

On November 13 it was the Foreign Secretary's turn to speak about the case in the House of Lords. He said that he knew the case fully and was satisfied that justice had been done. He repeated the statement that my views on the Berlin problem had played no part in the case. Taxed with the question why I had not been told of the complaints he said : 'I do not think that in every case it is right that the officer should be shown the source of a report or should know what is exactly in the report. But I will have another look at this case in the light of what the noble Viscount (Viscount Alexander of Hillsborough, Leader of the Opposition) has said. I think that I should make the distinction here that it is not a dismissal from the Service, but a retirement.' Lord Chorley suggested that the unfortunate thing about the case was the impression it gave that, in order to succeed in the

Diplomatic Service, you have to be a 'yes' man; but Lord
Home did not agree. He ended with some sharp criticism of
the press.

At this point Mr Anthony Greenwood returned to the attack
in the Commons. He put down ten questions of a highly searching nature. Some of the answers, when they appeared in written
form some days later, were most significant. Unfortunately,
because they were answered in writing, no supplementary
questions could be put. To the first question Mr Peter Thomas
replied curtly that no White Paper would be issued since Lord
Home's statement had showed that it was not necessary. In
my view the real reason was quite different. To have published
all the documents in the case would have meant revealing to
the public the petty and vindictive character of many of the
accusations, which had later to be withdrawn. The other
nine questions were answered with a great deal of obfuscatory
verbiage. Mr Thomas 'regretted' he had made a misstatement
about the date of the inspector's visit to Cyprus. He admitted
that Sir Christopher Steel had made no complaints to me
about my work in Berlin but said that 'when Major-General
Dunbar was appointed British Commandant (in May 1962)
Sir Christopher Steel, in the light of what he knew about relations between Mr McDermott and his military colleagues,
thought it necessary to say to Mr McDermott that the General
was in charge and must be loyally supported.' This, I am
sorry to have to say, is not accurate. What Sir Christopher
Steel actually did, as I have said earlier, was to congratulate
me on my collaboration with Major-General Delacombe and
add that the new Commandant would depend heavily on me.

Mr Thomas next confirmed that the one and only report
on my work by Major-General Delacombe was the adverse
one of May 22, 1962, made after he had left Berlin and
retired from the army. Mr Thomas repeated his adverse com-

ments but did not say that they had had to be very much
modified in the memorandum eventually sent to the Secretary
of State, as a result of my refutation. He next mentioned two
adverse reports by Sir Christopher Steel, in December 1961,
and January 1962, and said that they were made known to
me in the letter of June 1. This again was not correct: I had
never heard of the second one until Mr Thomas mentioned
it on this occasion. Inaccuracies of this kind were becoming
common form and I was getting used to them. In his next
two answers he stated that no complaints had been
made in writing against me by any members of my staff
either to Sir Christopher Steel or to the Foreign Office; and
that no indications of dissatisfaction were given to me by Sir
Harold Caccia or Sir Francis Rundall between July 1, 1961,
and June 1, 1962. On the next question Mr Thomas displayed
once more his weakness over chronology. He was asked what
opportunity I had been given of clearing myself of any charges
or complaints before the letter of June 1, 1962. He answered
with a long rigmarole about the procedure followed *after* that
date. In effect his answer was: 'none'. His last three answers
repeated the point that as I was 'retired' and not 'dismissed'
Foreign Service regulation Number 12 about disciplinary
offences did not apply and so the Foreign Office were under
no obligation to face me with the charges and complaints
against me.

There the Foreign Office case rests. You could drive a coach
and horses through it. Both Labour and Conservative
members, from both Houses, have made enquiries of the
Foreign Secretary indicating their dissatisfaction. I am most
grateful to them all: to Lord Silkin, who though very busy as
Deputy Leader of the Opposition found time to receive me

and go into the matter, and no less to those personal friends in both Houses who have taken it up. The Foreign Secretary has made no further statement, and it seems clear that he remains adamant. I personally have no wish to flog it any further; I am not a man with a grievance. I have described the whole matter as objectively as I can : to put it mildly, I must say again that it is all extremely odd. But is it enough to put it mildly?

There are very serious implications. My personal fate is the least important aspect of the case. I do not think it right that my dismissal should have been sprung on me as it was, or that none of my superiors made any move to see me in spite of my twenty-six years of service. I am bound to suspect some personal animus against me, a suspicion confirmed by the extraordinary dodging from story to story by Foreign Office spokesmen and the misstatements and inaccuracies into which they have so frequently fallen. The most likely explanation of their conduct seems to me to be that a small number of highly placed officials, faceless people (though I know their faces), had decided to get me out. They used the flimsiest pretexts : the first *Observer* story in April 1961, and the Cyprus Inspector's report. I have related what followed : not only were Steel and Delacombe shortly to sever their connections with Berlin and end their careers in the ordinary way, but mine was ended much more abruptly the following year. It is most striking that no Foreign Office spokesman has said a word about my work in Berlin, my relations with our allies, with the Berliners and with the rest of the Diplomatic Corps. Nor did any Foreign Office representative take the trouble to come and see for himself on the spot. My readers must draw their own conclusions. The Foreign Office's attitude has led some to speculate that I was pushed out as a sop to Adenauer because he did not like my political views, and even that it was all done to please the Americans. I heard later that the Pentagon had expressed astonishment at the whole affair. So had my many friends in Berlin. For me there is still a missing link.

More serious, however, than my personal fate is the reflection which the handling of the case has cast on the present Conservative Government. I was only one of quite a crop of resigners and retirers about this time, the others more distinguished than myself : Sir Hugh Foot, Sir Patrick Renison and Mr Thomas Galbraith. All of these contributed to a widely held opinion that this Government had become rather careless about the way in which it wielded the power it had held too long.

Even more serious is the effect which the case has had on the reputation of the Foreign Service, both with the general public and with members of the Service. It is, after all, an absolute principle of British justice that it must not only be done but be seen to be done, and also that a man is innocent until he is proved guilty. I am quite sure that some consciences very high up in the Foreign Office are uneasy. I believe, too, that because the authorities followed the regulations to the letter they think they are in the clear. It is true that no Act or regulation said in terms that I should be shown the charges; but equally no regulation said that I should not. The authorities chose to follow the easy way out. They must have been aware that my name was included in a list, unofficial but widely circulated throughout the Service in 1961, of twenty-four members who were either at the top already or were considered most likely to get there. But have they any idea, I wonder, of the warmth of the support that I have received from members of the Foreign Service? I have had large numbers of sympathetic letters from all over the world. One of my colleagues, almost in tears, said he wished he had been the victim instead of myself!

I have a great affection and admiration for the Service, and I want to see it prosper in the modern world. It will not do so without changes. The whole personnel and administrative side, enormous, unwieldy, inefficient, needs an overhaul. It seems at present possessed of a sort of *folie des petitesses*. A business efficiency firm, if one were put in, would cut out the growing bureaucracy, speed things up and encourage a more human and personal approach. There will be resistance to this on grounds of security, though these are not paramount in this particular context. Fortunately, a high-powered committee under Lord Plowden has been set up to examine the structure of the Service. Its report is to be confidential; but I hope that as much of its criticism as possible will be made public.

Towards this prospect of reform I can only hope my case may prove to have been useful. Has anyone ever asked the question : if the application of these regulations leads to such results, can they be good and just? For if the question is not asked and if reforms are blocked, then I fear my case will be more likely to deter people from entering the Service and displaying therein both initiative and energy. What is needed, on the policy-making as well as the administrative side, is more original, searching and constructive thought and action.

Chapter 12

MY PLAN FOR BERLIN

Did I succeed in my mission, such as it was, in Berlin? Diplomacy is not really a matter of success and failure, like the winning or losing of battles. But I believe I played a modest part in keeping the situation steady and the morale and position of the Berliners and the allies in Berlin unimpaired; and this was, after all, the year in which Berlin took her third great knock, in the shape of the Wall, after the bombing and Soviet invasion during the war and the blockade of 1948–9. Could I have achieved more? Given time and some better senior British colleagues I believe that I could; and I shall now explain my plans for improving the situation.

Why is Berlin so important to the West? After all, we defeated the Germans in the two world wars which they started; many people in the West, particularly perhaps in Britain, do not much like Germans. Indeed, large sections of people in Federal Germany are unlikeable: self-seeking politicians, over-prosperous industrialists, narrow provincials. Although Nazism as such is dead—and we must give much credit for this to Dr Adenauer—it stands to reason that many Germans who are active in many spheres today must have been Nazis and may not have changed their minds about that doctrine. Moreover, there are rather frequent signs that the democratic spirit there is far from strong. I am not a great believer in the infallibility of public opinion surveys, but in one carried out in Federal Germany in 1962 fifty-six per cent of all who answered declared themselves 'for democracy' : rather thin. Some of these opted for a 'dictator democracy' [*sic*], others for 'democracy only in foreign affairs'. Only one per cent were for dictatorship *tout court*; but—ominous again— twenty-six per cent gave no answer. In Federal Germany today there is no doubt that a number of men wield power who, to say the least, are not devoted to democracy, and some of them might be prepared to advocate using military force to reunify Germany. In practice, of course, this would lead to the nuclear smashing of Germany by the communists. It is true that the Berliners are much more likeable than the other Germans on the whole, and one can admire the forti-tude with which they have stuck it out against constant heavy pressure. But it is not *pour leurs beaux yeux* that we must regard Berlin as so important.

Is it outstandingly important as the future capital of a reunited Germany? I do not believe so. A united Germany, after all, existed only for a short time before cracking up as a result of its attempts to expand by force. Only for a very few years did it include all the German-speaking provinces, and that was when Hitler had brutally seized Austria and Czechoslovakia; but, important though the principle of self-determination doubtless is, that episode represents a realisation of it with which we want nothing to do. Berlin was for a while the somewhat remote capital of a country where pro-vincial feelings were very strong : the Rhinelanders often disliked the Prussians, the Bavarians the Hanoverians, and so on. These feelings are still strong in Federal Germany today, as the name might suggest. In Bavaria, the Rhineland and elsewhere you meet many Germans today who would frankly rather not hear much of Berlin. They are happy to pay their bit towards the subsidies that help to keep Berlin going; but beyond that they are not much interested. Of course, no Federal German politician could afford to speak like this, but that is another matter. Berlin, out in the region where Slav blood mingled a good deal, and rather unsatisfactorily, with Teutonic, and now less than half as far from Poland as from Federal Germany, was never a beloved capital and centre of culture in the same way as London, Paris, Rome or Madrid. Now that it is in an isolated situation with little prospect of becoming the capital of a reunited Germany, at least for a very long time, the official line is that it is much desired as a capital by both West and East Germany for the time being, and by both for the reunited future. In practice East Berlin is already the capital of the GDR; and whatever our feelings about the Wall may be, it confirmed and strengthened this state of affairs, which is recognised by the USSR and her followers. It is important also to appreciate accurately the position of West Berlin. This is considered by the Federal Government as equivalent to a *Land* or province; but in fact and in law it cannot both enjoy that character and the protection of the occupying powers at the same time. Consequently, Berlin has her own Government, as I have described; and Federal legislation, including legislation affecting foreign affairs, is only extended in its application to Berlin after approval by the three Western allies. In practice it is not all extended to Berlin.

Is it the wealth of Berlin that makes her so important to the West? Hardly. West Berlin is a prosperous city, owing to her inhabitants' hard work, her subsidies received chiefly from Federal Germany, and the protection afforded by the occupying powers. But so long as Germany is divided she will remain a city without an immediate hinterland, and these three forms of support will continue to be essential to her even though the last one may be arranged on a different basis, as I shall later suggest.

One key question is that of the reunification of Germany. We all know that Germany is divided because of the blunderings of her own Nazi government : I say this with no pleasure in the punishment which she has brought on herself, but simply to get the facts in perspective. Both the West and the communists agree in principle that Germany should be reunited in due course, that is to say when arrangements satisfactory to all concerned can be made. But what are the real prospects? It is a mere pipe-dream to suppose that the Russians will withdraw their forces in the foreseeable future. Why should they? They do not regard East Germany as a dependably communist state if left to its own devices, any more than they so regard their other satellites; and East Germany provides them with a very useful forward military and political position, and will continue to do so, in the present epoch of mixed nuclear and conventional strategy. Moreover, although the Russians exaggerate the degree of Nazi sentiment in Federal Germany, they are quite right to fear the consequences of nuclear arms in German hands, and I have no doubt at all that that is where many Federal German politicians aim to have them. It was impressive to see that President Kennedy showed himself so clearly opposed to such a development in a public statement in the autumn of 1961. Moreover, there are a great many people in the NATO countries who would be very happy if Germany were never reunited; and there is no doubt that this includes quite a number of Germans themselves, in both the Federal Republic and the GDR. In the other communist countries, and in many uncommitted countries, this feeling is even stronger and more widespread.

There is a good deal of loose and wishful thinking about the GDR. It is occupied, by right of conquest, by Soviet forces—though the communist line is that they are there by treaty rights. It is a communist German state, run by Germans. Probably some ten per cent of the population are real communists; plenty more are happy to help them actively along, and there is no lack of Germans ready, for instance, to build the Wall, keep it in repair, man it, and shoot fellow-Germans on the orders of their own authorities. Many people outside Germany seem to think that all this is done either by Russians, or under direct pressure from them in every instance; this is simply not so. There is good reason to suppose that Kruschev would have preferred not to have the Wall, and was talked into it by the German leader Ulbricht and his German colleagues. The Wall and the death-contrivances round the perimeter are revoltingly brutal; but things of a comparable nature have been done in other communist satellites. Since the not very large uprising of 1953 in the GDR the population, amounting to seventeen millions, have taken little action to liberate themselves, though admittedly three million have defected to the West. They have shown none of the ingenuity, spirit and determination of other countries in dealing with their own collaborators or the occupying power. As for Ulbricht, he is not beloved, but he holds the reins of power firmly, seems to move around safely in public, and is altogether an excellent and efficient agent for the Russians. I cannot imagine that they will sacrifice him, except conceivably in their own good time (nature may get him first—he is in his late sixties); nor that his replacement will necessarily be any better. I doubt therefore whether it is realistic for the West to demand a 'Gomulka-type' government in the GDR as part of a bargain, though I see no

great harm in trying it on. In the economic sphere the GDR
does not flourish as she should with her considerable agricultural and industrial resources; and this is in part due to
bad working morale caused by unpopular communist
methods. A specific example is agriculture, where the people
have refused to collaborate properly in the measures of col-
lectivisation that have been imposed. But in the first place I
do not think that the Russians give high priority to her
economic progress : their main interest is that conditions shall
not get so bad that they produce a political explosion.
Secondly, there would seem to be little danger of this; for the
standard of living in the GDR is still the highest in any communist country including the USSR, as Ulbricht was allowed
to remark publicly in 1962. It is often reported that the
GDR is grinding to a halt in the economic sphere; this is
simply not correct.

To sum up this part of the argument, I see no intrinsic
difference between the condition of the GDR and that of
other satellites, such as Hungary, Bulgaria or Roumania,
whom we have always recognised. For what it is worth, the
GDR's Warsaw Pact allies—the USSR and the other European satellites—have no deep affection or trust for her, in
spite of their political, economic and military collaboration.
Also, although the Federal German Government adheres to
the principle, under the so-called Hallstein doctrine, of not
recognising states who recognise the GDR, it makes an exception in the case of the USSR. This is a considerable exception,
made for reasons of *Realpolitik*, and I think that this uni-
lateral principle of theirs could be further relaxed not only
without harm being done but probably to good purpose.

To consider the question of Berlin's importance more posi-
tively, she has some three and a half million inhabitants;
and the fact that one and a quarter million have come

under communist control makes it all the more important for the West to look after the rest. Secondly, our civilian and military representatives are there by absolute legal right agreed by the Russians at the end of the war; it may be, as I shall suggest, that a better, because more up-to-date, legal basis can be established by a new agreement, but that gives the communists no justification for simply declaring the West's established rights to be abolished. On a side issue of some importance, in practice the Russians can, of course, abolish their own rights if they wish, and renounce the responsibilities arising from their rights; and we are put in a rather silly position when we insist they cannot. This is one of several aspects of the allied position that needs modernising.

But above all the importance of Berlin is political and strategic. It was not the West who built the Iron Curtain; but it is there, and the Cold War results from it. Berlin is not only a great symbol of Western civilisation; it is a living, dynamic, loyal part of it. This has nothing to do with its tactical military significance, which both sides agree is small. Kruschev compared it to a bone in his gullet, and dismissed its intrinsic importance with a wave of the hand. At the same time the communists have maintained throughout the years their unrelenting pressure on it, and will continue to do so. To put it negatively, if the communists were to have their way—even to the extent of West Berlin becoming what they call a 'free', demilitarised city—they would achieve a success comparable with their take-over of China; NATO would almost certainly collapse; the hands of those West German politicians favouring a policy of appeasing the USSR—the so-called 'Rapallo' tendency—would be much strengthened. It would be a tremendous communist breakthrough.

The West, then, must prevent this at almost any price; some would say, at any price. The crucial question here is,

are we going about it in the best way open to us? I am convinced that we are not, and that an agreement with the communists which could ease matters not only for the West but
for the communists too is perfectly feasible. It calls for some
hard and realistic thinking.

The intolerable thing about Berlin from the Western
angle is that the situation threatens the world with war
—nuclear war. This was the case in 1961; it will be so again
before long. It is not the communists who make this threat; it
is the West who are driven to it as a result of the unsatisfactory nature of their position in Berlin and of their diplomacy. For over a year endless discussions went on between
the West and the Russians on Berlin; absolutely no progress
was made. Now this may look satisfactory; we are thus pre-
serving the *status quo*, and our rights, in Berlin. But in the
first place, we are able to do so only because the Russians
agree to allow us and for the present take no firm action to
dislodge us : to that extent we are dependent on the Russians.
Secondly, any Western statesman attempting to deal with, say,
Cuba or Laos or the Congo is always bedevilled by the latent
threat represented by Berlin. Thirdly, as part of this picture,
the West's position in Berlin is not very dignified, and we can
almost never take the initiative there. But, above all, the weaknesses of our static position in Berlin and our static diplomacy drive the West to utter the most portentous threats.
Surely we can find a method of negotiating that is less
dangerous, and more skilful, than this? I cannot agree with
those public commentators, and the numerous allied officials,
who think that the game of chasing one's own tail, while
brandishing the nuclear weapon, is the highest and best form
of diplomacy.

Kruschev has threatened ever since 1958 that he will sign

a peace treaty with the GDR, doing it jointly with the Western powers if they wish it, but without them if not. He has laid off, in spite of his 'ultimata', because he considers he can harass the West satisfactorily without taking this step, which in its complete form of denying all their rights in Berlin might, as he well knows, lead to war. After the Cuban crisis Kruschev must have considered taking the plunge. He decided, for the time being, on a wiser course; but there is no knowing when he may change his tack. It is up to the West to use this time to good effect, and not to fritter it away. The treaty, when it comes, may of course not go the whole hog, or not immediately, but it will at least be a considerable further step towards handing over West Berlin, the allied representatives there and the access routes to the tender mercies of the GDR.

I conclude that the Western allies' policy of waffle has had its day; I think there is still a chance of agreement with the communists if we take action soon, on the following lines.

1. The Western powers and the Soviet Union would agree that the long-term aim is the reunification of Germany (both sides have stated this to be their policy) and the agreements would be subject to review in, say, twenty years.

2. The present German frontiers would be recognised as definitive. This is just plain commonsense, as there is no advantage in 'waiting for a peace treaty'. This step represents no concession by the West as a whole : nor really by Federal Germany since her only hope of regaining her 'lost territories' in Poland and Czechoslovakia lies in a world war, which in its turn would smash Germany. But it would please the communists.

3. The GDR would be recognised as a separate state—as indeed it already is: a German state ruled by Germans. Britain and her allies do a lot of trade with it; Federal Germany does a very great deal of trade. The East German

authorities already control ninety-five per cent of the people going into and out of Berlin, including, of course, all the normal, i.e. non-official, nationals of the Western allies, and are recognised by all concerned for these purposes. In addition, there are numerous administrative and technical matters, such as the running of the railways throughout Berlin and across the GDR to West Germany, in which the East German authorities' responsibility is fully recognised by all. Herr Brandt himself favours an extension of these contacts, as he has said publicly from time to time. As for the international political implications of such recognition, in the first place it need not imply approval any more than does our recognition of the régimes in other satellites; secondly, it need not confer any great advantages on East Germany—the Bulgarian, Roumanian and Hungarian régimes, for instance, have hardly achieved any great standing as a result of recognition by the West; and finally it would mean recognising a state of affairs which will almost certainly exist for a very long time, for the reasons already explained. This, of course, would be a concession by the West; it would have the advantages of being realistic, and of pleasing the communists. It would also have the advantage that we could send diplomatic and consular missions into the GDR and develop contacts with the inhabitants. It would admittedly pose a problem for the Americans, who tend to use recognition as a mark of approval rather than a simple facing of facts, as witness their policy over China. But I dare say that they could find ways and means of overcoming this if the bargain as a whole was sufficiently attractive. I do not, incidentally, consider talk of *'de facto'* recognition very profitable. In law it is doubtful whether it really means anything. And in practice the West already accords this to the GDR, so that it is hardly a new factor in the case.

4. Berlin would be recognised as the separate entity it already is. It has nearly three and a half million inhabitants. In practice we should no doubt have to rest content with West Berlin : this has two and a quarter million inhabitants, or far more than many already independent states. She would make agreements with any powers she chose —except the two Germanys—to station their troops in reasonable numbers in the city. This would be similar to the agreements between the GDR and the Warsaw Pact countries. No doubt West Berlin would choose the Western allies, so that in effect our forces would stay as at present but on a new basis, improved because agreed between the West and the communists, unlike the Occupation Status today. This would ensure that Berlin would be really independent and not merely 'free' in the communist sense. United Nations (non-NATO) troops on their own would be worse than useless and would lead only to chaos and communist intervention. It is true that Mr Kruschev has grumbled at the presence of the allies' troops as constituting an 'aggressive NATO base', but he does not believe a word of it, and chiefly wants to get rid of the Occupation Status. An advantage for the West would be that the allies would be represented in Berlin by ambassadors in the usual way, who would be independent of the ambassadors in Bonn and who would control their own forces in Berlin. It would represent a different type of concession by each side, and should give West Berlin every chance of continuing to prosper as a civilised community while removing some of the irritation caused by the fishbone in Kruschev's gullet. After all, the seizing or even subversion of an independent member of the United Nations, as Berlin would become, would be a highly dangerous operation for the communists, especially in the presence of ambassadors from scores of states all over the world. Their presence would also have some effect

in shaming the communists into better behaviour over the Wall. Berlin would, of course, be free to go on receiving material support from the West, and also to develop trade and other relations with the GDR and with any other state.

5. The four powers would agree on guarantees for the access of their representatives, both civilian and military, to Berlin. The numbers would, as now, be very small compared with the total traffic between Berlin and elsewhere. East Germany could derogate sovereignty in this respect to the USSR without any cause for complaint—such arrangements are often made between allies. This would be a reasonable arrangement, not fully satisfying to the GDR perhaps but entirely practical.

6. Some important agencies of the United Nations would be moved to Berlin. Mr Kruschev has shown some signs of agreeing to this. The Economic and Social Council or the Food and Agriculture Organisation might be suitable; the Human Rights Commission particularly so. If, as is likely, they were confined at first to West Berlin, they would still be first-hand witnesses of the Wall and all that goes with it, and might be expected to exercise some beneficial effect on the East Germans. This move would also benefit the economy of West Berlin and of the GDR if they chose to be sensible about it. The idea of moving the entire United Nations headquarters seems less practicable.

7. The three German states would become members of the United Nations. This would give advantages to both sides, since at present not even Federal Germany is a member but merely has observers there. They would all three adhere to these agreements; indeed, any number of other states would be welcome as guarantors.

A suggestion which I favour less, as it seems to me less practical and more propagandist in character, is that the West should summon a peace conference of the fifty-two states who fought against Germany. This has a certain attraction on paper, and Brandt has in his time put it forward, though with no great emphasis. But it is most unlikely to achieve anything, and for the reasons I have given I consider that the time for producing paper tigers out of the hat is past.

There is also the idea of referring the whole problem to the United Nations. This might be done by either side. I think it is very unlikely to resolve the impasse. Various other ideas have been put forward by the West for dealing with different aspects of the problem, such as setting up an international body of thirteen nations to supervise the access routes. Though these ideas vary in quality most of them suffer from being piecemeal suggestions, or cumbersome, or not very realistic: as often as not I think they are mere ingenuities designed to keep the conversations with the Soviet Government going. As I have already said, that is fine as far as it goes, but we should not delude ourselves into thinking that it goes anywhere near a solution which can be agreed with the communists.

I believe on the other hand that my combination of suggestions preserves the interests of all parties. It has the great advantage that it could remove Berlin for a period, and possibly a long period, from the very dangerous position it has occupied for so many years, and will otherwise continue to occupy for many more. Of course, prestige is much at stake. But I believe these ideas would save faces all round. More important, questions of war and peace are at stake: both sides should be happy for a lull on this particular front. For these reasons I think Kruschev could accept an arrangement on these lines if he set his mind to it. Some friends have asked me: even if Kruschev did accept, wouldn't the agreement be only another scrap of paper? And what happens in twenty years' time? I think that if something is not done soon we may all become scraps of débris as a result of Berlin, or at best the Western position there may be ignominiously whittled away; and I think that the very fact of Kruschev agreeing to such arrangements would bring a sense of relief almost everywhere in the world. Let us think later about such important, but not absolutely vital, questions as Berlin's relations with the Common Market.

The 'McDermott plan' has had considerable publicity on both sides of the Iron Curtain, and most of it has been favourable except in the case of comments by Federal German ruling circles. I described it recently, and answered questions on it, at a gathering of diplomats representing the West, the communists and the uncommitted countries which the Quakers had assembled in London; and I was gratified to hear favourable comments from all quarters including American and Hungarian representatives.

The crucial question obviously is this: is it likely that Kruschev could accept an arrangement on these lines, and if so why? I believe the answer is that he could; and I will try to explain why, in the setting of East-West relations as a whole, in the next chapter. I will only say here that the more reasonable tone recently adopted by Ulbricht, together with Kruschev's lack of haste over Berlin, seem to me to provide the opportunity for sensible discussion. It is not good enough for the West to make no effort in response to these gestures from the East. This will discourage them; and we may be certain that the stiffer line over Berlin will return sooner or later. Moreover the concessions by the West which I have suggested are wasting assets. We should use the present breathing-space to the best effect.

Indeed, I think that for some time we may have more difficulty in persuading our NATO allies, France and Federal

Germany, to agree to a settlement on these lines. But Adenauer and de Gaulle will disappear one day. A man like
Schroeder might have the courage to take the plunge; and if
the SPD come to power the position would be more hopeful
still. De Gaulle or his successors might also be willing, though
for different reasons of their own. In any case, these are not
good reasons for the West, represented by the USA, Britain
and many sensible allies, to give up the effort now.

Meanwhile, I believe that almost everyone, in either camp,
who thinks about Berlin would agree with my view that it is
well worth a visit, as the Berliners themselves say; it might be
worth a battle; it is not worth a war.

Chapter 13

BERLIN'S PLACE
IN EAST-WEST RELATIONS

The extraordinary Cuban affair has been described as showing a new pattern in power politics; and I think this is right. Since the future of all of us depends on how that pattern works out, it is worth giving it some thought. Amongst other things, it is important to know where Berlin comes into it.

There are still intelligent people who confuse the rule of law, which is basic to international dealings even if interpretations of it differ widely, with the *status quo*, which is not in any way sacrosanct; which, on the contrary, is being changed all the time whatever some powers and individuals may wish, and which we should all be constantly trying to improve. What the West (indeed the world) needs is a dynamic policy with a firm base to it—which does not, of course, mean mere action for action's sake.

The history of the last fifty years well shows how nations, like families, rarely enjoy the same status for long : some improve their position, others decline. The two world wars, started by the Germans with such inadequate forces and unforeseen results, have accelerated this process with the result that what might have been two hundred years of history have been crammed into a quarter of the period. In 1914 Britain and her empire stood first; France and hers second; Germany was coming up fast and wishing to go faster still: Russia was large but rotten; the USA were nowhere in the race. By 1919 things had changed a great deal, but not catastrophically from the Western point of view. Britain and France still stood where they had, but their strength had been sapped; the USA had proved her worth but had few worldwide ambitions; both Germany and Russia—by now the USSR— appeared shattered. In the twenty years between the wars the relative position of both Britain and France gradually declined; Germany, thanks to the concentration of the Nazis on military strength, once more felt powerful enough to challenge the world; the USA's economic power grew, while her political and military power increased at a lesser pace; the USSR laboured on through purges, inept government and economic inadequacy while at the same time increasing her political influence by the spread of communism round the world.

It was not until towards the end of the last war that the USA took over the general leadership of the West. That war led to the end of the British and French empires, though the commonwealths that have succeeded them still wield considerable influence. Germany was shattered but has made a recovery which can be called good if only partial, since she is divided into three sections. But the real phenomenon has been the USSR : after losing tens of millions of her people during the war and being beaten back to Leningrad, Moscow and Stalingrad, she has recovered to the extent of being far more powerful than the Russian empire ever was, and, for most purposes, ranks equal top in the world league.

If there are decisive turning-points in history, the Potsdam conference was one of them. When President Truman told Stalin and the others that the USA had the atomic bomb and would use it, he might almost as well have dropped it on the table. From that moment the Cold War was on. All available Soviet resources were devoted to catching up : the building up of military power, an aggressive and expansionist foreign policy combined with a stubborn refusal to collaborate with the West ('*nyet*'), economic resources so that the bomb came first and the other interests of the people nowhere, scientific resources, of course, and world-wide espionage.

It is undeniable that for a few years the USA was in a position to quell the USSR by the use of the bomb, though of course this policy was never seriously considered by the United States Government. The ravages of the German war and the insecurity of those few years before the Soviet Union got the bomb herself have deeply marked the character of Soviet policy and its exponents, and it will be a long time before the effects disappear. But this extraordinary concentration of effort in Stalin's last years and since has had some very important by-products as well as the main one. The Soviet Union's general economic effort has flourished, as has her intellectual and scientific effort in general, even outside the nuclear sphere; but her standard of living is still low.

Now, therefore, the Soviet Union is far more dangerous than she was before. First, in terms of crude force, she has all the nuclear power she needs for all purposes. I do not agree with those, often scientists, who draw fine distinctions between the numbers and the range of the H-bombs possessed by the USA and the USSR respectively, and conclude that the USA has a significant lead. A lead she may have, but it does not signify : each has the power to smash the other completely, and much of the rest of the world as well, and that is that. This situation has only been reached, as a result of Soviet progress, fairly recently; from now on we must live with it. In passing, Soviet achievements in space have the most massive military implications, just as the USA's do. In addition the USSR has very large 'conventional' forces, though she is weak in transport. In spite of the improvement in her standard of living she devotes, and will continue to devote, all that is required to her military effort.

But along with this impregnable force goes a somewhat new and improved style of diplomacy. We must never for a moment forget that her objectives remain as before : the supersession of capitalism by communism everywhere in the world. But the application of Marxist methods, the outstanding characteristic of which is their flexibility and adaptability, is now being pursued in a far cleverer and, for us, more dangerous, way than in the last days of Stalin. The Government that allowed the poet Yevtushenko to visit Britain and talk objectively and unfanatically about communism, is the same as that which slipped the nuclear missiles into Cuba. Certainly, travel in the USSR is easier than it was; the people are friendly and more open than they were; it is possible to have detailed discussions of world problems with Soviet diplomats, scientists and others without banging into the *nyet* brick wall. The basic reason is that the USSR is now in a position of great strength. But her two chief characteristics remain as before : she is expansionist, and the days of her weakness and insecurity are not forgotten.

Certain dominant factors seem clear to me. Kruschev does not want nuclear war because at the very least the USSR would suffer so much that she could probably never recover enough to pursue her worldwide aims. It would in fact benefit only others. I do not say that he would in no circumstances fight such a war; if that could be said, the problem would be easier. But unless subjected to threats of a sort which he must regard as intolerable I do not think he will go into one. Of course, his judgment of what is intolerable may not always tally with the West's. But these considerations apply also to the USA. Secondly, Cuba has provided one more example of a well-established characteristic of Soviet policy: the Soviet Government is not fussy about 'losing face' and if one of its deep probes meets with really determined opposition, it is prepared to withdraw. Incidentally, as often as not it has meanwhile achieved part of its objective. Thirdly, something has gone seriously wrong in the communist world, and shows every sign of getting worse: Soviet relations with China. We must not exaggerate. They are very broadly on the same side; and it is possible, though not I think likely, that relations could be patched up. But communism is not proving a success in China, and is being pursued along lines which the Soviet Government considers wrong. The result is that the Chinese Government tries to distract attention by criticism of the Soviet Government and by a constantly aggressive attitude towards almost everyone. China, as Mao remarked in an unguarded moment, does not fear a nuclear war for she could lose more than the entire population of the USA or the USSR and hardly notice it. And she will have her own nuclear weapon shortly. The violently critical Chinese reaction to Kruschev's withdrawal from Cuba, together with Kruschev's failure to support China against India and indeed his tendency to support India, have shown up the rift in a blindingly clear light. Various recent Communist Party conferences have emphasised it still more. It is not too fanciful to suggest that the USSR might consider it right to take forceful measures against her great Chinese ally at some appropriate moment. (That is strictly a problem to be sorted out amongst the communists themselves.)

Fourthly, I imagine that Kruschev reckons the Cuban

adventure well worth while. Chiefly, he has probed Kennedy and got an accurate answer : he will of course probe again when and where he sees a chance. The effort and expense have been considerable, but not inordinately so. Some sort of undertaking has been extracted from the United States Government to leave Cuba alone for a while; personally I hope that Kennedy will treat this one flexibly. Kruschev has asserted ruthlessly his control over his satellite Cuba, *pour encourager les autres.* Some weaknesses have been revealed in the support given by the Western allies to Kennedy over the whole affair. Kruschev himself has appeared to the not too intelligent as a reasonable angel of peace, having of course very nearly caused world war in the first place. Thoughts in the West have been seriously turned towards overall negotiation; we cannot lurch from one terrible crisis to another indefinitely. Moreover, Kruschev himself may still want to go to the United Nations sooner or later; and he may be in need of more backing than he already has against China. In sum, I believe he may soon be ready for negotiation on many things at the highest level. He said some time ago that he would be if matters got desperate enough; and now he deliberately in Cuba, and the Chinese for their own reasons, have brought things to this pass, even though there is a temporary lull at present.

Should we in the West now accept the challenge of serious negotiations on all problems? I believe that we should. The United States Government understands very well the facts of the nuclear balance of power. Twice within about a year the Americans have been manoeuvered into threatening nuclear war : over Berlin in the autumn of 1961, and over Cuba. Kennedy has taken the measure of his leading opponent; he has found him formidable but not unmanageable. Kennedy has emerged as the saviour of the world from nuclear war;

and yet he has resisted *hubris*. He could negotiate from great strength and with iron confidence with the object of finding some area of agreement to encourage people in both West and East to get down to peaceful, if highly competitive, co-existence. Korea, Indo-China and most recently Laos were all right as far as they went; but they all involved fighting and bitterness. Any fighting now is liable to be far more danger-ous; and, on the positive side, what a gain for the whole world it would be—except perhaps for communist China—if some measure of agreement could be reached without fighting first. This has been done over Cuba, at the risk of a fearful crisis; we should aim to do better in other contexts.

Where do the Western allies stand over all this? Another clear lesson of the Cuba affair has been that when it comes to the crunch the Americans do well to keep their closest allies informed. But they cannot be expected to consult them at every step. I find this quite acceptable. To take ourselves, the facts of the present world situation are not as attractive as were those of fifty years ago; but they are the facts. Our political experience and skill, our position at the centre of the Commonwealth, our economic resources and our world-wide defence effort make us far from negligible as an ally; and so far from neglecting us the United States pay great attention to us. We are the only power in the world which is a full member of the three major 'Western' alliances. These are NATO, including eleven West European states, two Middle Eastern (Greece and Turkey) and the United States and Canada; the Central Treaty Organisation, a decidedly more rickety affair, comprising Britain, Turkey, Iran and Pakistan, with the United States playing the major part though technically as an 'observer'; and the South-East Asia Treaty Organisation including Britain, France and the US again, plus Pakistan, Thailand, the Philippines, Australia and

New Zealand. Clearly, our defence resources are excessively stretched : a third-class army mainly in Germany and in penny packets elsewhere, and a first-class, but comparatively small, Royal Air Force and Navy. Nevertheless, it all helps to give weight to our counsels. I think that, without insisting that the USA should keep us informed at every turn, one of the chief services we can render is to put forward our views whenever appropriate and to back them up in any negotiations they may undertake with the Russians. We should also urge our other allies to adopt a similar attitude.

An important measure which we should take in order to increase the effect of our counsels in the Western alliance is to look deeply at the shape and methods of our defence effort and to take steps, however drastic, to improve it. I am myself convinced that we could save both money and manpower, and at the same time increase efficiency, by setting up a strong Ministry of Defence to take over the duties now performed by the three Service departments and some of those of, for instance, the Ministry of Aviation. Correspondingly, we should work rapidly towards a unified Royal Defence Force in which the unproductive rivalries and overlapping between the three Services would be eliminated and the energies thus released used for constructive purposes.

The value of France and Germany to the Western alliance is much more limited. They are well placed 'pieces of real estate' and they provide some useful conventional forces, but this is almost all (the French nuclear armoury is negligible, and I trust the Germans will never have one). Even so they tend to exploit their nuisance value more than we do our more straightforward kind. Perhaps things will improve before long. The smaller allies are generally loyal and useful, and less likely to cause difficulties for the Americans and the Western cause. Britain could probably help more effectively if she were a member of the European Economic Community, which is one good reason for trying to become one.

I have referred to the political and strategic situation, and, before specifying the problems which might be discussed between the two sides, it is worth defining it further. It arises from the expansionist tendencies of the Soviet Union, plus their fear of insecurity, since the end of the war. The communists have taken several forward steps of importance since then. The greatest was the winning over of China, though that has now brought its own complications. The other significant one was the subversion of Czechoslovakia. On the periphery of continental Asia they have advanced in Korea, Viet-nam and, up to a point, Laos. All round the land mass of the Soviet Union are these forward positions of some, though diminishing, defensive importance in the military sense but at the same time of considerable importance as political launching-pads. In Europe there is the Warsaw Pact consisting of the USSR and all her European satellites. But the · Soviet Union's main offensive and defensive military power consists in her missiles, of which she has a full armoury in all sizes and ranges, with nuclear-powered and -armed submarines coming along fast. Behind these stand a large army, navy and air force. The West's reply is a series of forward bases ringing the Soviet Union on every side, plus the political and strategic alliances on which they depend; and, more fundamentally, the United States armoury of nuclear missiles, not least those carried by the Polaris submarines and the Strategic Air Command. Both sides are increasing their capabilities in space. As with the communist side the West's defences are backed by more 'conventional' air, army and naval forces. The main burden is borne by the Americans everywhere, since only Britain and France of all her allies have a nuclear capability, and small at that. But as regards

forward bases, Britain, Germany and France contribute considerably in Europe; Britain in the Middle East; and Britain
again in South-East Asia.

That is the setting. Is it satisfactory? Or should we try to
negotiate something better with the communists? Surely we
should make every possible effort. In 1961 Berlin nearly led
to the loss of millions of lives, in 1962 Cuba brought the
danger nearer still. The West's worldwide defence arrangements are very expensive and not very flexible; they are liable
to be leap-frogged, politically if not militarily, by the communists—as in Cuba. For most practical purposes the two
sides are evenly matched; but time does not stand still, and
though the West might possibly improve its position by inten-
sifying the Cold War I do not personally see how, and the
balance might very well tip the other way. Let us put prestige
and 'face' in their proper places and get down to hard negotiations; we need not automatically turn down proposals, or
parts of them, because they come from the other side, as there
is a tendency to do. Let us aim at solid results, and at the
same time use the negotiations themselves as a deep probe,
just as the communists do. Let us for once resist the temptation of saying, time and again, before negotiations begin that
they will be long and difficult. Let us aim sincerely at some
quick successes, with all the relief they would bring to human
beings everywhere.

Now for the subjects of negotiation. It is obvious that
everything to do with nuclear armaments is of the highest
importance; but equally most aspects of this set of problems
are so fundamental that they are the most difficult to settle.
Two aspects seem to me to be reasonably negotiable : a sus-
pension of nuclear testing (which has already happened once)
and an agreement not to extend in any way the area where
nuclear weapons are held. In Europe this would be an appli-

cation of the Rapacki plan which proposed setting up, under inspection, a nuclear-free zone in Federal Germany on the one hand and the GDR, Poland and Czechoslovakia on the other. Federal German objections would have to be overcome, and could be if the major nuclear powers were determined enough. Even more important, nine tenths of the world would be entirely free from the need to strain their economies by efforts to win a place in the nuclear race; they would not become tempting targets for the stronger nuclear powers; and they would be no more defenceless relatively than they are at present. Common sense demands such an agreement. Some form of control and, if possible, sanctions would have to be devised, either through the United Nations—and Kruschev's agreement to some UN inspection in Cuba was a good sign— or through the major powers. But even a partially satisfactory agreement on these lines would be well worth while. A valuable development of this, either at the same time or later on, would be an agreement to widen the nuclear-free zone. The Americans have made a start by announcing their intention to withdraw such weapons from Turkey. The more complete the nuclear armoury on each side becomes, the less important in fact are these forward nuclear bases.

I hope that the preparations for such negotiations are in train. It looks as if good work is afoot behind the scenes already. The West must be prepared for every contingency. Certainly, what is pejoratively called 'secret diplomacy', although it is in fact no different from the confidential discussion so necessary in business, for example, should be used whenever appropriate. If on occasions the West uses verbiage as a stalling tactic they should be very sure they are doing so on the merits of the case, and not as a sort of reflex action.

Looking round the world we could find many areas—in South-East Asia, Africa and Latin America—where sensible agreements could be made on the methods of propagating the rival ideologies; competitive co-existence will go on, willy-nilly, but it should be possible to devise measures to avoid unduly dangerous situations. A non-aggression pact between NATO and the Warsaw Treaty Powers should be feasible and useful. Finally, one pressing major problem could, I am convinced, be solved on the lines I have suggested : that of Berlin. This would be a clear, concrete achievement, and a highly encouraging example. The world, East and West, would heave a great sigh of relief and people could turn their attention to more profitable matters.

Chapter 14

THE FUTURE

I am often asked whether I expected war to come over Berlin while I was there. I did not. I have no doubt that the American Government meant every word when they said that they would fight for Berlin's freedom if necessary. Equally I have no doubt that America's allies, including of course the British, would not have followed her along that line except in the most extreme circumstances. Certainly, in discussions with people who were in Britain at that time, I have met no one who seriously expected war, though some political leaders and newspapers adopted a fairly bellicose line. I am sure that the French and Federal German Governments would have done everything possible to avoid it. But above all Kennedy's show of strength was well calculated to impress on Kruschev that he could go just so far and no further. He made it clear that he understood the significance of the *salami-taktik* of cutting off apparently harmless slices one by one from the Western position, and that at a moment of his own choosing he would cry halt and mean it. The whole contest was a dress rehearsal for the Cuban crisis a year later. I may add that I did not expect war then either.

Since the Cuban crisis relations between the USA and the USSR have been moving, slowly but steadily, in the right direction. There is no doubt that a probing exchange of views is going on all the time confidentially between President Kennedy and Mr Kruschev. That in itself is most important. Kruschev carried out faithfully the first part of the Soviet withdrawal from Cuba; now he is carrying out the second part. Kennedy has undertaken to withdraw the American missiles—which were obsolete anyway—from Turkey. The introduction of a Polaris force into the Mediterranean will in any case greatly improve the West's deterrent posture in that part of the world. An improved approach has been made on both sides to the question of a test ban, though little real progress is to be seen so far.

Finally, Kruschev and Ulbricht have spoken in far gentler terms than before about the possibility of an agreement on Berlin. In particular, Kruschev has now suggested—as I forecast some time ago that he would—that the Western forces should stay on in Berlin. He qualifies this in two ways : they should stay for a time, and they should stay as UN forces. This is a significant move in the direction of my own plan. I have suggested a period of twenty years' validity for it; and if Kruschev mentions five or six, the difference is surely negotiable. Secondly, my plan proposes that the Western forces (or any others, Federal Germany excepted, on which the State of Berlin wished to agree with the powers concerned) should stay on an exactly similar treaty basis to that of the Warsaw Pact by which Soviet forces are 'temporarily stationed' in the GDR. Here again, the difference is surely negotiable.

The great dialogue itself is, therefore, going well at present. Unhappily, however, the West is passing through a period when it is its own worst enemy and repeatedly inflicts wounds on itself. This must affect Kruschev in two ways. First, he can see little reason for hastening an accommodation so long as his opponents are obligingly disrupting their own strength. Secondly, and more basically, he must feel inclined to wait and see how far that weakening process will go, for if it goes far enough his own line will be that much tougher.

The Nassau meeting of President Kennedy and Mr Macmillan seems to have been an almost total disaster. First, British dependence on the United States for her most important weapons was rudely emphasised by the new terms imposed for Skybolt. The subsequent agreement on Polaris was no bad thing in itself, but in this context it again emphasised the degree of our dependence. Then the catastrophically handled offer by Kennedy and Macmillan of nuclear favours to de Gaulle gave him the opportunity to decree, from his high horse, that America and Britain were not Europe and perhaps never would be. He and his old friend Adenauer would now mould Europe along their own lines: it would become a third force equal in power to the 'Anglo-Saxons' and the communists.

We reacted too gently to the machinations of the 160-year-old couple. De Gaulle has a madness which the French call *'la folie des grandeurs'*, in the plural, because it goes inexorably on from one megalomaniac activity to the next. Adenauer too is a dictator for half of every day, and gaga for the other half. These facts make it unlikely that their schemes will all work out as planned. If they did, we should be well out of their 'Europe'. But while the whole world wishes to see France and Germany in amity, one cannot help cynically remembering that the last time they pledged themselves to it for ever was in 1938, when they were represented by M. Bonnet and Herr Ribbentrop. There has been much conspicuous osculation between the two old gentlemen, but it would not be surprising if, before long, the kissing had to stop.

Kruschev has already waved aside the idea of the Third Force as ridiculous. But there is one feature of the Franco-German agreement which he must take very seriously indeed; and I regret to say that the same applies to one of the other results of the Nassau meeting. This is the possibility that, in one way or another, the Germans will get their hands on nuclear weapons. This could happen by deliberate French action; or under the NATO multilateral agreements now proposed by the USA. Any possibility that, for instance, a German submarine captain might command an operational Polaris vessel for even a few days will be regarded with great gravity by Kruschev; and personally I see his point. I fear that any such development may cause a serious setback to the improvement of East-West relations. We cannot prevent France from giving Germany some nuclear weapons, horrifying though the prospect is. But let us not try to pre-empt this particular market in order to please the German Government. That would be both ridiculous and very dangerous. I trust that this project will come to nothing.

These recent developments strengthen the reasons for the policy I have advocated. Britain should back America in all her enterprises, with the right and duty to argue against those which seem misguided such as the multilateral nuclear plans and the stationing of 55,000 British troops in Europe. She should do all she can, without trying to interfere beyond her powers, to help forward the Kennedy-Kruschev dialogue. She can make a special contribution of her own here, as Kruschev said to Roy Thomson and the hundred-and-fifteen other British businessmen in his private party a short time ago. For one thing she can expand her trade with the Soviet bloc, and encourage the Americans and others to do so. This would be profitable both economically and politically : under the latter heading it would, apart from its more constructive results, help to spike the de Gaulle-Adenauer guns. Secondly, Kruschev said on the same occasion that Britain could play a special part in solving the Berlin problem, and I am sure that this is true. Let us help the Americans as much as we can on this, and take the initiative ourselves while the atmosphere is more favourable. Sooner or later it will take a turn for the worse.

The collapse of the Brussels negotiations on British entry into the Common Market and the signing of the Franco-German treaty have raised in an acute form the future direction of British foreign policy. We need to take a long cool look at Europe, realising that it is we and America and Russia who are the three strongest powers on the Continent. Our principal enemies are the Communists, de Gaulle and Adenauer. Of these the Communists are amenable : they are ready to bargain realistically with the West on matters extending far beyond Europe. De Gaulle remains in power from a bland assumption of his indispensability and a love of power. He is maddened by our close collaboration with America and by his own inferior military position. Adenauer did much for German democracy after the war, but in 1959 he could not bear to step up to be President, even though he could have continued to supervise the political scene. He too, following de Gaulle's lead, has said he is not interested in Britain entering the European Community. Both he and de Gaulle resent the memory of their liberation at the hands of the British and Americans. It is so much harder to forgive a favour than to forget a wrong.

First things first. If we approach world problems in this way, the European problem will fall into its proper place.

February, 1963.